Infant/Toddler Caregiving

A Guide to

Cognitive Development and Learning

Edited by

Peter L. Mangione

Developed collaboratively by

WestEd and

California Department of Education

with funding from

Carnegie Corporation of New York

  WestEd

Publishing Information

Infant/Toddler Caregiving: A Guide to Cognitive Development and Learning was developed by WestEd, San Francisco. See the Acknowledgments on page x for the names of those who made significant contributions to this document.

This publication was edited by CDE Press, working in cooperation with Peter L. Mangione, WestEd, and Janet L. Poole and Mary Smithberger, Child Development Division, California Department of Education. It was designed and prepared for photo-offset production by the staff of CDE Press, with the cover and interior design created and prepared by Paul Lee. Typesetting was done by Donna Varee Kurtz and Anna Boyd.

It was published by the California Department of Education, 1430 N Street, Sacramento, CA 95814-5901. It was printed by the Office of State Publishing and distributed under the provisions of the Library Distribution Act and *Government Code* Section 11096.

ISBN 0-8011-1055-6

Ordering Information

Copies of this publication are available for $18 each, plus shipping and handling charges. California residents are charged sales tax. Orders may be sent to California Department of Education, CDE Press, Sales Office, 1430 N Street, Suite 3207, Sacramento, CA 95814-5901; FAX (916) 323-0823. Mail orders must be accompanied by a check (payable to California Department of Education), a purchase order, or a credit card number, including expiration date (VISA or MasterCard only). Purchase orders without checks are accepted from governmental agencies only. Telephone orders will be accepted toll-free (1-800-995-4099) for credit card purchases only.

A partial list of infant/toddler caregiving materials available for purchase may be found on page 75. In addition, an illustrated catalog describing publications, videos, and other instructional media available from the Department can be obtained without charge by writing to the address given above or by calling the Sales Office at (916) 445-1260.

Photo Credits

The California Department of Education gratefully acknowledges Sheila Signer for the use of photos that appear in this publication.

Notice

The guidance in *Infant/Toddler Caregiving: A Guide to Cognitive Development and Learning* is not binding on local educational agencies or other entities. Except for the statutes, regulations, and court decisions that are referenced herein, this handbook is exemplary, and compliance with it is not mandatory. (See *Education Code* Section 33308.5)

Prepared for printing
by CSEA members

Contents

A Message from the State Superintendent of Public Instruction

More infants and toddlers than ever before are spending significant amounts of time in child care programs. Yet despite growing public awareness about the critical importance of the first three years of a child's life, many parents still have great difficulty finding safe, healthy, and intellectually engaging programs with well-trained caregivers for their infants and toddlers. As a result, the California Department of Education has embarked on a partnership with WestEd to create the Program for Infant/Toddler Caregivers (PITC), a comprehensive training system with videos, caregiver guides, and trainers' manuals.

This document, *A Guide to Cognitive Development and Learning*, is one part of these resources designed to improve the quality of infant/toddler child care. It was written by experts in the field of early learning, development, and care. The information presented here focuses on intellectual development during infancy with an emphasis on activities that are naturally interesting to infants and toddlers. The document also presents information about the importance of responsive care, the environment, and appropriate play materials.

We encourage child care programs to use this document to guide caregivers in their efforts to support early learners in mastering the lessons of infancy—lessons that are crucial to later success in school and life. Thank you for your commitment to the well-being of the infants and toddlers in your care.

JACK O'CONNELL
State Superintendent of Public Instruction

About the Authors

*M*arc H. Bornstein is Senior Research Scientist and Head, Child and Family Research, at the National Institute of Child Health and Human Development. He holds a Ph.D. from Yale University. Bornstein received the C. S. Ford Cross-Cultural Research Award from the Human Relations Area Files and the B. R. McCandless Young Scientist Award from the American Psychological Association (APA). He was a J. S. Guggenheim Foundation Fellow, and he received a Research Career Development Award from the National Institute of Child Health and Human Development (NICHD). Bornstein has held academic appointments at the Max-Planck-Institut für Psychiatrie in Munich, the University College in London, the Institute for Behavior Therapy in New York, the University of Tokyo, and the Sorbonne in Paris. He is the coauthor of *Development in Infancy* and *Perceiving Similarity and Comprehending Metaphor* and is the general editor of the *Crosscurrents in Contemporary Psychology Series*. His other works include *Psychological Development from Infancy, Comparative Methods in Psychology, Psychology and Its Allied Disciplines* (vols. 1–3), *Sensitive Periods in Development: Interdisciplinary Perspectives, Interaction in Human Development, Handbook of Parenting,* and *Cultural Approaches to Parenting.* He also edited *Maternal Responsiveness: Characteristics and Consequences* and coedited *Developmental Psychology: An Advanced Textbook, Stability and Continuity in Mental Development,* and *Contemporary Constructions of the Child*: *Essays in Honor of William Kessen.*

Helen G. Bornstein, an environmental lawyer and freelance writer, holds a B.A. in mathematics from Barnard College, an M.A. in anthropology from Columbia University, and a J.D. from the University of Pennsylvania. Bornstein has conducted research in developmental psychology at Yale University and at the Max-Planck-Institut für Psychiatrie in Munich, Germany.

Tiffany Field, Ph.D., a professor of pediatrics, psychology, and psychiatry at the University of Miami Medical School, is also the director of the Debbie School Infant, Toddler, and Preschool nurseries at the University of Miami. Field is the recipient of the American Psychological Association's Boyd McCandless Distinguished Young Scientist Award and of the National Institutes of Mental Health (NIMH) Research Scientist Award. In addition to being the author of many papers for journals, she has edited over a dozen publications on high-risk infants and on stress and coping throughout development and is the editor of a paperback series, *Clinical/Developmental Issues*. She has recently written a book titled *Infancy* and is the editor of a paperback series, *Clinical/Developmental Issues*.

J. Ronald Lally is the Director of the Center for Child and Family Studies, WestEd, San Francisco, which created the Program for Infant/Toddler Caregivers for the California Department of Education. The caregiver training system provides videos, written materials, and technical assistance. Lally is the coauthor with Ira Gordon of *Learning Games for Infants and Toddlers*; coauthor with Alice Honig of *Infant Caregiving: A Design for Training*; and coauthor with Kuno Beller, Ira Gordon, and Leon Yarrow of *Studies in Socio-Emotional Development in Infancy*. Dr. Lally also directed the Syracuse University Family Development Research Program, an early intervention program for low-income children (from birth to age five) and their families. He is currently directing the longitudinal follow-up study of the effects of the Syracuse program.

Theodore D. Wachs is Professor of Psychological Sciences at Purdue University. He received a Ph.D. in 1968 in Child Clinical Psychology from George Peabody College. He has had visiting faculty appointments at the Institute of Child Development, University of Minnesota; York University in Toronto; and Indiana University. In addition, he was awarded an NIMH Post-Doctoral Fellowship for advanced study at the Child and Family Branch, National Institute of Child Health and Human Development. His research interests center on the study of environmental influences, on infant and toddler development, and on the interaction of individual characteristics and environmental influences. He is the author of *The Nature of Nurture* and coauthored several books, including *Early Experience and Human Development* and *Assessment of Young Developmentally Disabled Children*.

Acknowledgments

This publication was developed by the Center for Child and Family Studies, WestEd under the direction of J. Ronald Lally. Funding for this document was generously provided by the Carnegie Corporation of New York. Special thanks go to Marc H. Bornstein, Helen G. Bornstein, Tiffany Field, Theodore D. Wachs, and Peter L. Mangione for their contributions to this document; to Karla Nygaard for editorial assistance; and to Janet Poole and Mary Smithberger, Child Development Division, California Department of Education, for their review of the content. Thanks are also extended to the members of the national and California review panels for their comments and suggestions.

The national panel members are T. Berry Brazelton, Laura Dittman, Richard Fiene, Magda Gerber, Asa Hilliard, Alice Honig, Jeree Pawl, Sally Provence, Eleanor Szanton, Yolanda Torres, Bernice Weissbourd, and Donna Wittmer. The California panel members are Dorlene Clayton, Dee Cuney, Ronda Garcia, Jacquelyne Jackson, Lee McKay, Janet Nielsen, Pearlene Reese, Maria Ruiz, June Sale, Patty Siegel, and Lenore Thompson.

Material that appears in the sections on caregivers' practices was drawn from the Child Development Associate (CDA) Competency Standards for Infant/Toddler Caregivers and Family Day Caregivers. Finally, "Developmental Milestones of Children from Birth to Age Three" in Section Three and "Appropriate and Inappropriate Practices" in Section Four were excerpted from *Developmentally Appropriate Practice in Early Childhood Programs Serving Children from Birth Through Age 8,* edited by Sue Bredekamp (Washington, D.C.: National Association for the Education of Young Children. 1987). The material is used by permission from the publisher.

Introduction

Studies consistently show that a baby learns most and fastest—and will likelier remember what he learns—when *he* can control what's happening. . . . it's those experiences *he* chooses (not necessarily those chosen *for* him) that help him learn fastest and most completely.

Evelyn B. Thoman and Sue Browder
Born Dancing, pp. 109–110

Experts in early development and care have increasingly recognized the importance of giving infants and toddlers the freedom to make choices. Yet many articles and books urge caregivers to be in charge of the kinds of stimulation that infants and toddlers experience. Caregivers have often been told to stimulate or "teach" babies early in life and to do special activities or else the children will miss key learning experiences. In addition, countless numbers of educational toys and materials have been designed to teach babies specific lessons. This push to teach and control the stimulation that infants and toddlers receive is now being balanced by a growing awareness of the effect of too much stimulation on babies. Indeed, the research literature questions the value of teaching infants and toddlers, especially when teaching interferes with children's natural learning activities. Thoman and Browder suggest that in optimal learning situations, babies are in control; and formal teaching usually takes control away from them.[1]

But if being in control is beneficial for babies, does the caregiver have any role to play in early cognitive development and learning? The answer is an unqualified *yes*. In fact, the caregiver plays a special part in the learning and development of an infant or toddler. The caregiver's role includes being responsive to the infant, interacting as a partner, setting up the environment, and providing interesting and appropriate materials. These topics are among the ones that will be covered in this

[1] Evelyn B. Thoman and Sue Browder, *Born Dancing: How Intuitive Parents Understand Their Baby's Unspoken Language and Natural Rythms.* New York: HarperCollins Publishers, Inc., 1988, pp. 109–110.

guide to infant/toddler caregiving. Missing from this list is teaching. The caregiver and the infant are usually occupied with far more important matters than the content of a specific didactic lesson. How the naturally occurring actions of infants and toddlers contribute to their early development is the subject of this guide.

Does avoiding teaching mean that caregivers should simply let babies be? Or should caregivers initiate activities and perhaps even stimulate infants? The answer to these questions is—it depends. Too often the debate on infant stimulation has been reduced to all or nothing. Some experts say that stimulation from caregivers is good; others, that it is bad. But caregivers cannot help but stimulate babies, even if they try not to do so. In caring for infants and toddlers, caregivers naturally talk, provide guidance, structure the environment, and nurture children. All of these actions stimulate babies directly or create conditions that do so. Infants and toddlers need this stimulation from caregivers to develop and thrive.

The matter is more complicated than simply deciding whether to stimulate infants and toddlers. For example, when is an infant ready for stimulation? Is the stimulation simple enough for the infant to follow and learn from? Is it interesting to the infant? Is it too loud, too bright, or too fast? Answers to such questions have to be considered from the perspective of the infant. And for that perspective to be understood, the infant's reactions to stimulation have to be observed. The infant has to be allowed to act and react. Letting the child be in control of stimulation is the key to being able to (1) understand his or her interests and reactions; and (2) decide whether a certain type of stimulation is appropriate or inappropriate.

Giving infants and toddlers opportunities to be in control not only benefits their development but also enables the caregiver, through observing children making choices,

to discover how to respond appropriately and thereby support early cognitive development and learning. Knowing what to look for in the actions of infants and toddlers is helpful. Sometimes the actions of infants may appear unimportant to the casual observer, but the children are learning on their own terms—the best approach available to them. In "Discovery in Infancy: How and What Infants Learn," J. Ronald Lally illuminates how simple actions (for example, sucking on a toy) are profoundly important to infants. With an emphasis on the actions and needs of infants and toddlers, the chapter gives an overview of development during infancy, in particular the processes of learning and discovery. The caregiver's response to an infant's actions, especially when the child is expressing a want or need, is also important.

The relationship between responsive caregiving and cognitive development is addressed by Marc and Helen Bornstein, in "Caregivers' Responsiveness and Cognitive Development in Infants and Toddlers: Theory and Research." They define *responsiveness,* examine characteristics of responsive caregiving, and summarize research on the developmental impact of responsive caregiving. Part of being responsive to infants, the authors state, is knowing when to engage in social interaction with them.

In "Supporting Cognitive Development Through Interactions with Young Infants," Tiffany Field describes how the level of alertness and activity of infants affects their ability to learn through interacting with an adult. A caregiver who is sensitive to such factors will be better able to engage an infant in increasingly prolonged interactions. Field also suggests how caregivers can adapt their behavior to an infant's emerging capacities.

In addition to appreciating the significance of the naturally occurring actions of infants and toddlers, being responsive to their needs and interests, and becoming partners in interaction with them, caregivers influence early development through the environments they create and the materials they make available to children. Theodore Wachs, in "The Physical Environment and Its Role in Influencing the Development of Infants and Toddlers," explores the impact of the physical environment on the cognitive development of infants and toddlers. Wachs discusses factors to consider in setting up environments for infants and toddlers and offers practical guidelines for selecting materials and toys.

The articles described previously are followed by three sections that provide additional information on cognitive development and learning during infancy. Section Three presents a list of developmental milestones related to cognitive development. This list gives a general picture of the capabilities, interests, and activities of children during the young, mobile, and older periods of infancy. Of course, children vary tremendously in the extent to which they manifest these milestones. Section Four, "Appropriate and Inappropriate Practices," spells out developmentally appropriate and inappropriate practices in caring for infants and toddlers. These practices are from material excerpted from *Developmentally Appropriate Practice in Early Childhood Programs Serving Children from Birth Through Age 8,* which was edited by Sue Bredekamp and published by the National Association for the Education of Young Children. Practices selected to be included in this guide are particularly related to cognitive development and learning in infants and toddlers. The last section of this guide, Section Five, "Suggested Resources," provides a list of printed and audiovisual resources for trainers and caregivers to refer to for additional information on the cognitive development and learning of infants and toddlers.

Some topics in this guide are covered to the exclusion of others. Two key topics that have received limited treatment are caregiving routines and culture. The lack of attention given to these topics is not meant in any way to diminish their importance in early cognitive development.

Such routines as feeding and napping are central in the care of infants and toddlers. For many reasons experts say that routines are the curriculum from which infants learn. During routines children learn about their bodies, their needs, their likes, and their dislikes. As they eat, they discover the taste and texture of different foods. If performed in a consistent, organized way, caregiving routines make life predictable for infants and toddlers. Predictability in a child's daily life supports both social-emotional and cognitive development. The child can begin to understand and appreciate order in his or her world. Throughout this guide opportunities for one-to-one contact with a caregiver are cited as important in early development, and routines often give an infant a chance to have one-to-one time with a caregiver. The role of routines in early development, including cognitive development, is given in-depth coverage in *Infant/Toddler Caregiving: A Guide to Routines,* one in a series of guides developed by the Program for Infant/Toddler Caregivers.

Early development and care, of course, occur both inside and outside the child care program. The role of the child's family and culture in learning is crucial. Interaction with infants and toddlers and caregiving routines are handled uniquely in each culture. Depending on their cultural background, some families may believe that their babies learn through doing, while other families may believe that their babies learn through observing. These cultural differences are fundamental and sometimes subtle. A respectful openness to an infant's or toddler's culturally based approach to learning and discovery is an essential part of caregiving. The role of culture in cognitive development and learning during infancy is addressed in a companion guide entitled *Infant/Toddler Caregiving: A Guide to Culturally Sensitive Care.*

This guide explores the contribution of the naturally occurring activities of infants and toddlers to their learning and development. During virtually every waking moment, infants are learning and making discoveries, particularly when they have the freedom to choose the focus of their activity and exploration. Whether banging a rattle on the floor or looking for an object or participating in a routine such as eating, infants are involved in an important activity. Infants and toddlers benefit greatly when they have a caregiver who is sensitive and responsive to their needs and interests, who creates developmentally appropriate environments, and who introduces activities that encourage the children to explore freely and be in control of what happens. The following pages offer many insights and ideas for caregivers seeking to provide that kind of support to infants and toddlers.

Section One:
Cognitive Development

Cognitive Development: Vision Statement

The caregiver provides activities and opportunities that encourage curiosity, exploration, and problem solving appropriate to the developmental levels and learning styles of children.

Exploring and trying to understand the world are natural and necessary for children's cognitive or intellectual development. As children learn and grow, their thinking capacities expand and become more flexible. Adults should support and guide this process by responding to children's interests with new learning opportunities and to their questions with information and enthusiasm. Cognitive growth also requires healthy development in other areas: physical growth and development of motor skills, a secure emotional base, and positive social interactions.

Young infants (birth to nine months) begin cognitive or intellectual learning through their interactions with playful, caring adults in a secure environment. Some of their early learning includes becoming familiar with distance and space relationships, sounds, similarities, and differences among things, and visual perspectives from various positions (front, back, under, and over). Such learning can be reinforced by describing to infants what they feel, hear, touch, and see.

Mobile infants (six to eighteen months) actively learn through trying things out; using objects as tools; comparing; imitating; looking for lost objects; and naming familiar objects, places, and people. By giving the infants opportunities to explore space, objects, and people and by sharing children's pleasure in discovery, adults can help children become confident in their ability to learn and understand.

Toddlers (sixteen to thirty-six months) enter a new and expansive phase of mental activity. They are beginning to think in words and symbols, to remember, and to imagine. Their curiosity leads them to try out materials in many ways. Adults can encourage this natural interest by providing a variety of new, open-ended materials for experimentation. They can create a supportive social environment for learning by showing enthusiasm for the children's individual discoveries; encouraging them to name things and talk about their experiences and observations; asking questions that have more than one answer; and encouraging the children to compare and contrast objects, sensations, and events.

Discovery in Infancy: How and What Infants Learn

J. Ronald Lally

Our personhood begins in infancy, a stage rich with activity.[1] An understanding of how young children form lasting relationships, start communicating with others, and bring order to their world can turn your time with the child you care for into an adventure. You see a personality emerging, a mind struggling to make sense of experience. You see the child in the early stages of creating her or his reality—bringing meaning to each event, each action.

With what looks like crude and primitive actions, infants give structure, order, permanence, and predictability to their experiences. Infants work not as passive recorders but as active artists and paint their versions of reality. New meanings and new ways of finding meaning emerge from slight alterations in old meanings and in old ways of finding meaning. To watch infants engage in this process is to watch growth itself. If caregivers watch carefully, they will witness a mental life that is constantly changing, becoming more complex, yet at the same time maintaining continuity with the past.

This chapter contains information about how infants think and what they think about—information that should make it easier for you to care for infants in ways that foster their development.

Three Points To Remember

When working with children, caregivers need to remember three major points:

1. *Children grow and develop at different rates and with different temperaments.* This fundamental truth is supported by research studies and theory in child development. So do not pay too much attention to the child's age in discussions of particular traits. Certain behaviors appear earlier for some children and later for others. Remember, too, that infants not only develop at different rates but also have different likes and dislikes. One infant, for example, enjoys sucking more than another infant does. Another infant shows signs

---

[1] In this chapter the term *infant* is used to mean infants and toddlers from birth through age two.

of pleasure from being cuddled and does not suck as much as the first one. Still another infant likes to be out of clothes and blankets more than most. They are individuals when they come into the world, and they remain individuals as they grow.

2. *A child's intellect, emotions, and body do not develop separately.* The child grows and learns holistically, not in compartments. Motor, language, moral, intellectual, social, and emotional skills, attitudes, and stances blend to form the personal style of each child. Each area of development enables and influences development in other areas.

Motor ability influences what children can explore, emotions flavor the language that they use, and mental pictures influence emotion. For example, at between eighteen to twenty-four months of age, most children have fairly good control of their body. They can walk and run, use their small muscles for

detailed work, and are starting to control their bowels and bladder.

At the same time children are developing skills in language. They know many more words than they can correctly say; and they are beginning to express desires, wishes, and resistance to the wishes of others.

Intellectually, these children are beginning to figure things out, and they have some basic mental symbols and ideas. They are starting to pretend and to understand concepts of past and present. At the same time their viewpoint is ego-centric—they see things almost exclusively from their point of view. They have begun to see that choice of action is possible.

All of these traits help to mold children's views of life. Increasingly, they experience themselves as independent of mother and father: They stand on their own feet, walk in their own way, think their own thoughts, express themselves in their own words, and become capable of many acts through their own skills.

3. *Although adults obtain clues from infant behavior, all adult thought about how infants think describes infants in adult terms.* Adults have labeled various aspects of infant development, but those designations are just labels. Words like *autonomy, shame, initiative, independence,* and *guilt* are adult constructs that can illuminate certain aspects of infant behavior and development. Yet these constructs can be deceptive if they lead to the belief that the experience of infants is the same as what comes to the minds of adults when they

hear and think about such words as *autonomy* or *shame*.

Very young infants experience the world without knowledge of words and without the clarifying abstractions of adults. For example, infants do not experience trust as adults do. Trust is an adult concept that can be evaluated as good or bad, strong or weak, present or absent. The infant may be building a sense of trust that is not thought about or evaluated. Evaluation is the key to understanding the difference between infant and adult thinking. Young infants do not consciously reflect on experience, rate behavior, or judge themselves. They just live. Young infants do not realize anything about the process of development. They just develop. The older infant and toddler begin to evaluate but not with the specificity of the adult. Toddlers are more spontaneous and far less introspective than adults.

Infants and adults have different abilities, and infants cannot experience the world in the same way as adults do. Similarly, adults can no longer experience the world as infants do. Sometimes, the adult view does a disservice to the infant. That is, most adults feel that their views and skills are better than those of infants and that the adults' view of life is more real than the infants.' This way of looking at infants invalidates the infants' experience as "less than" the adults' experience— one that should be worked on by adults and changed rather than given time to develop. This view leads adults to try to shape infants, rush them through infancy to "more important" stages of life, push them

to reach an adult's understanding of the world, and teach them. This view can interrupt important infant work and impose inappropriate demands, requests, and expectations. It can lead to insensitive and inappropriate caregiving.

Understanding the Thoughts of Infants and Toddlers

This exercise will help you understand infants. As you do it, try to feel the difference in quality and style of behavior between an infant and an adult. Close your eyes and point to where you think your mind is. This request may seem silly, but please do it. Most likely, you will point to a place on or near your head. Adults do this because of the cerebral nature of their understanding. If young infants were asked to point to their minds and they were capable of understanding the exercise, they would most likely point to their tongues or fingertips.[2] Infants learn through their senses. Their learning processes are much less abstract and also much less efficient than those of adults. The sense system of learning used by infants requires more time, movement in space, and energy than the abstract system used by adults. This difference between infant and adult behavior is a key to understanding the infant's view of the world. For the infant, understanding is mostly sensation; for the adult, mostly idea. The attention of young infants is mostly in the present, and their senses influence attention powerfully. As infants become older, their thinking processes gradually change.

---

[2] The comments made about infant "thought" in this chapter are based on the clues that infants give us about their thought processes through their behavior. We do not know how infants process information internally. From their actions we infer how they think.

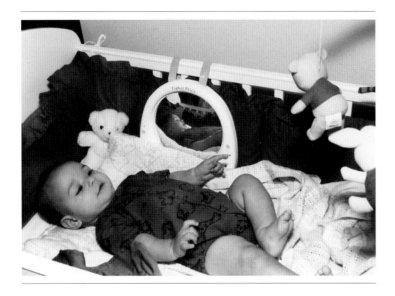

Look at how the process works. Place a mobile above the crib of a four-month-old to eight-month-old infant so that the infant can touch it with his or her feet. Watch as the child waves his or her arms and kicks his or her legs to move the mobile. Periodically, take the mobile away for a minute or two and then return it to the crib. Watch what the infant does to show recognition. When the child has become familiar with the mobile, he or she will act differently toward it when it is returned. You will notice that when the infant sees it, he or she will move his or her arms or legs toward the mobile, in a partial motion of what was done in the past to make the mobile move. This partial motion is a motor recognition symbol, a memory of the mobile and past actions taken on it. As the child gets older, the motor symbol becomes increasingly briefer, and only a slight foot movement in recognition may appear. Finally, the motor sign is difficult to see at all. The internalizing that the child's motor memory goes through offers a glimpse of the work of sense and motor connections in an infant's mental activity. This gradual movement from sense to symbolic recognition is an example of how infants develop in the way they act on, understand, and recognize things.

The Intellectual Activity of Infancy

During the first 24 months of life, infants are actively constructing their world. An appreciation of what they are doing will help you to act appropriately. This section of the chapter summarizes cognitive development and learning during infancy.

Use of Reflexes

At birth infants use the skills they have brought from the womb. Sucking, grasping, crying, hearing, seeing, and smelling operate at birth—as well as more specific reflexes, like the rooting reflex (turning toward an object that touches the infant around the mouth and grasping that object with the mouth) and the "Moro" reflex (the dropped infant raises its arms and grasps). Very young infants have other

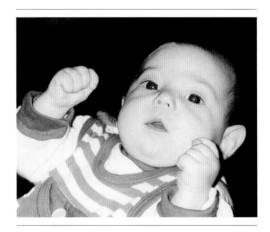

skills as well. Infants avoid brightness. They can see up close but not far away; and when they search with their eyes, their eyes move back and forth instead of up and down. They look at the edges of an object, not at the middle. They respond more to high tones when they are awake and to low tones when they are sleepy. They quickly come to recognize their mother's voice, identify smells, and prefer a mother's smell and voice to the voice and smell of a stranger. Young infants show preference for sweet liquids and for the human face. These skills are used for survival and for taking in information.

Altering Reflexes

As the infants develop, their use of reflexes changes. Gradually, sucking becomes sucking something satisfying to the taste and anticipating the nipple. Seeing becomes actively scanning the contrasts in light and dark. Hearing becomes listening—infants quiet their crying and body to be able to hear. The grasp changes to suit what is grasped. Unpleasant smells are avoided. Thumb sucking starts or increases as a chosen activity. Crying becomes a message that the parent can understand. By four months of age, the grasp has changed from a reflex closing of the hand when the palm is stimulated to a grasp that changes with the different objects or parts of the body grasped. The situation changes again when infants learn to keep their hands in view and try to look at things grasped and to grasp things seen. Early reflex behaviors have changed, infants have learned new skills through experience, and the skills learned have made the infants different.

Making Interesting Experiences Continue

At around four months of age, infants discover that experiences which they have caused by accident can also be caused on purpose. During this period they show a marked increase in leg kicking, arm waving, banging, rubbing, and shaking to cause things to happen. At the same time they start to put things into familiar categories. One of these categories might

be things to kick and see move; another, things to kick and hear make sounds. At about this time clear indications of intentional behavior appear.

Unquestioned Intention

Between seven and twelve months of age, infants show signs of unquestioned purpose. They move obstacles to get to a desired object and use tools to extend the impact of their body. At this time they also show signs of anticipation; for example, they learn from seeing their mother put all the diapering materials away that she is about to leave the room. Infants may cry even before she goes because they anticipate her leaving.

Fear of Strangers

Between seven to twelve months of age, infants learn to recognize those who have been caring for them and show signs of not wanting to be with strangers. They become able to recognize a familiar adult and clearly prefer that person. This period can be particularly trying for the employed mother and for families that use unfamiliar adults as baby-sitters. For the infants, however, this period represents an intellectual and emotional breakthrough that helps them to recognize friends, relax in their presence, and build more permanent relationships.

Active Experimentation

Around their first birthday, infants start to treat objects differently. During the infant's brief past, objects were to be explored and understood. The properties and functions of an object were of prime importance. Now, infants fool around with objects and look for less obvious uses. At this time they experiment with their own skills and seem to try to find new ways of doing things. One-year-old infants experiment and discover new ways of using tools and of getting what they want.

Insightful Learning

Around eighteen months of age, infants spend time inventing. They imagine ways of acting that will serve their purpose. Crudely, they figure out a way of taking new action. Piaget observed that his child continually opened her mouth at sixteen months of age while trying to get an attractive watch chain out of a matchbox (Ginsberg and Opper, 1969). The action seemed to help her "think" about how to open the matchbox. Such action is typical when children begin to manipulate symbols in the mind and to leave the sense world of infancy.

Discoveries of Infancy

Part of the excitement of caring for infants and toddlers is watching them become increasingly competent. So many lessons are being learned during infancy, and in such subtle ways, that adults often miss the lessons. It may be helpful for caregivers to cluster what is being learned into categories so that the child's learning

activities can be more easily understood. What follows is a clustering based on the films of J. McVicker Hunt and Ina Uzguris. They grouped learning activities that took place during the sensorimotor period as described by Jean Piaget into categories and placed them in order according to level of complexity and then placed examples of the activities on six films. To learn more about their system, one would find it helpful to view the films in the series "Ordinal Scales of Infant Psychological Development" (see the list of audiovisual materials in Section Five).

Discovery One: Learning Schemes

During the first two years of life, infants begin to put things in groups. They begin to develop familiarity with hard things, soft things, sticky things, light things, things that bounce, things that make noise, and so on. As they get older, they also learn to act differently with different kinds of things. Older infants

treat different objects in different ways. They will not try to make aluminum foil stick to a block without using scotch tape. They will also combine objects, put blocks in a container, or use a spoon to take sand from a sandbox. Learning the different properties of items continues into the preschool years. Infants touch, mouth, bang, pat, and throw things to discover the functions and properties of objects. Infants test the environment to see how it operates and learn new ways of acting in the process.

Discovery Two: Learning That Events Are Caused

Young infants do not know the connection between cause and effect. Often, they bite themselves and yelp in puzzlement and disbelief at the pain. They do not make a connection between the action and the pain. Cause-and-effect lessons develop in the same way as does the use of tools. Infants start to learn through their own body activity; and when they are about fifteen months old, they are actively searching for such causes as what makes a light go on or what makes a sound happen. For example, they increasingly experiment with cause and effect by playing with light switches, radio dials, doorbells, "pop-up" toys, and so forth.

Discovery Three: Use of Tools

During infancy, children learn to extend themselves through the use of tools. At first, infants take in information through sight, smell, touch, and so forth. They use sense tools. Then infants start to act on things with the body. They grasp a bottle, bring it to their mouth, and suck. Infants also learn to use adults; for example, by putting something to be opened or rewound into the hand of a caregiver. Infants use adults as tools for getting food, toys, and comfort. Finally,

infants use objects to help to get, hold onto, or explore things of interest; for example, standing on a box to reach the sink or pulling a leash to get a toy dog from under a table or chair.

Discovery Four: Object Permanence

From birth to about five months, the young infant does not realize that an object removed from sight and returned to sight is the same object. Repeated contact with familiar objects—a mother's face or a particular rattle—helps the infant to learn this lesson. When a child knows that things still exist even when he or she cannot see or touch them, the child feels a greater sense of the permanence of his or her world. This knowledge deepens the child's relationships with loved ones. During the first year of life, the infant learns that things are permanent. This understanding deepens and becomes more complex throughout childhood.

Discovery Five: Learning How Objects Fill Space

A good deal of infants' learning has to do with issues of space, density, distance, movement, and perspective. Infants bump into walls, crawl into corners, get stuck under tables, and reach for things beyond their grasp. They also do not understand distance and size, and they often have false impressions about how big an object is and how much space it will fill. Infants have difficulty understanding that objects can change shape and that objects can be manipulated into different spaces.

Discovery Six: Imitation

During the first two years of life, infants become increasingly skillful at imitation—a powerful learning skill. Early in life infants imitate their own behaviors. Gradually, they mimic what they see, starting with general body activity; and they become increasingly selective and precise with their imitation. A majority of infants' learning occurs through imitating caregivers. Infants learn to imitate sounds and actions. As infants move into the second year of life, they begin to imitate sequences of behavior. Eighteen-month-old infants combine sounds or imitate adults by using a cup, saucer, and spoon in pretending to drink coffee. Imitation is a powerful tool in learning socially appropriate behavior.

Facilitating Cognitive Development

The preceding six discoveries are learning themes that infants and toddlers experience throughout the first two years of life. As children grow, they discover more about a theme and gain a more complete understanding of how that knowledge can be used to their advantage. Children make these discoveries naturally. They do not need to be taught about cause and effect or about space and distance.

Rather than teaching infants and toddlers, you are to be an interested and interesting play partner. At times the infant will want to play an imitation game with you. The young infant may be most interested in taking turns sticking out tongues with you, while the older infant may be fascinated by a finger game and song you initiate. At other times the infant may learn about cause and effect by interacting with you. For example, if you are responsive, the young infant will begin to make the connection between his or her cry (the cause) and your coming close to comfort the infant (the effect). These are just some of the ways that your understanding and responsiveness are integral to the child's development. The chapters by Marc and Helen Bornstein and Tiffany Field in this guide give further insight into the influence of the

caregiver's action on the development of infants and toddlers.

In addition, part of facilitating children's development in general and intellectual development in particular involves offering choices of activities, respecting children's choices, and creating conditions for them to learn. Understanding the discoveries of infancy helps you (1) identify learning as it takes place so that you can avoid interfering with important intellectual activity; and (2) prepare materials and the environment so that the child will have a meaningful learning experience. The chapter by Theodore Wachs elsewhere in this guide provides rich information on environmental conditions that support cognitive development and learning in infants and toddlers.

When you look at infants as active learners who use their whole bodies (including their mouth, hands, feet, and skin) to discover the world around them, you see how important their actions are. Caregiving becomes more interesting when you see the discoveries that children are making each day and as you see yourself as a vital part of the children's fascinating enterprise of learning and discovery.

References

Ginsburg, Herbert, and Sylvia Opper. (1969). *Piaget's theory of intellectual development: An introduction* (Third edition). Englewood Cliffs, N.J.: Prentice-Hall, Inc.

Note: In support of this article, this addendum provides additional materials that have been published since the original publication of the guide.

Segatti, Laura; Judy Brown-DuPaul; and Tracy L. Keyes. (2003). Using everyday materials to promote problem solving in toddlers." *Young Children,* 58 (September).

Caregivers' Responsiveness and Cognitive Development in Infants and Toddlers: Theory and Research

Marc H. Bornstein and Helen G. Bornstein

*I*t was once commonly believed that responding too readily to a baby's cries would make the baby become fussy, or worse, a "household tyrant whose continual demands make a slave of the mother." Since that time, our knowledge about babies and infant care has increased significantly. We now understand that a baby's crying or smiling or reaching out sends a message about needs or likes or feelings, and it is only natural to respond to those signals.

Indeed, whether or not a caregiver responds to a baby's signals may be a matter of the child's survival. At birth and for a long time thereafter, human infants depend totally on adults to care for them. Not surprisingly, infants come equipped with a number of ways to communicate with their caregivers. The cry and the smile are two of the most powerful tools at babies' command. The cry tells a caregiver, "I'm hungry," "I'm tired," "I'm in pain," or "I need to be held." It brings the caregiver close to the child so that those needs can be met. The smile says, "I like to be near you," "I like when you play with me," or "I like to hear you talk." It also keeps the caregiver close and promotes interactions.

During the first year babies develop other signals or means of communicating that provoke responses from their caregivers. For example, they begin to coo and babble, they learn to direct their eyes to things and people of interest, and they learn to point and reach. Eventually, they learn to talk. Therefore, some of the signals most commonly used by infants to communicate with their caregivers include the following:

Distress vocalizing—Crying and fussing

Nondistress vocalizing—Cooing, babbling, and talking

Visual attending—Looking at objects and people in the environment

Facial expressions—Smiling and frowning

Body movements—Pointing at and reaching for objects and people

How caregivers should respond to these signals and what consequences, if any, a caregiver's responsiveness has for a child are the issues to be examined in this article. First, we will define responsiveness and identify its typical characteristics. Next, we will examine what effect responsiveness has on infant crying and what short-term and long-term effects responsiveness has on the cognitive development of infants. Then, we will look at how responsiveness influences growth and at sources of responsiveness in the caregiver. Finally, we will discuss how to become a more responsive caregiver.

What Is Responsiveness?

Experts define responsiveness to include a caregiver's verbal or nonverbal reactions to a child's signals. Responsiveness normally has the following three elements:

1. *Contingency*—meaning that the adult's action depends on or occurs in reaction to the infant's action
2. *Appropriateness*—meaning that the adult's action is conceptually related to the infant's action and is geared to fulfill the infant's need
3. *Promptness*—meaning that the adult's action follows the infant's action closely in time (so that the infant learns to associate the two)

Responsiveness in this context does not include a caregiver's act that just happens to follow immediately a child's act, nor does it include a caregiver's spontaneous stimulation of the child. That is because in neither of those two cases does the caregiver's act depend on or occur in response to a child's act. So, being

responsive means not just interacting with baby but being contingent, appropriate, and prompt too. For example, when a four-month-old infant turns to his or her caregiver and starts to coo, a responsive caregiver would make eye contact with the child and coo back—"have a conversation." If, after a time, that same child starts to fuss or averts his or her gaze, the responsive caregiver knows that the activity has ended. Responsive caregivers listen to children's signals and then adjust their behavior contingently, appropriately, and promptly to respond to those signals.

Researchers who study responsiveness actually decompose it into three separate but related events:

1. Infant action
2. Caregiver response
3. Effect on the infant

This analysis provides the researcher with a framework from which to take a closer look at the interaction and its effect

is usually in terms of "social soothing"; that is, talking to, patting, and holding the baby. Thus, while crying, an infant is most likely to experience contact with the caregiver and soothing social interaction. When caregivers respond to an infant's coos and babbles, they themselves typically vocalize, often imitating the child's sounds. When they respond to an infant's attempts at exploration, they generally help the baby to become oriented to the objects being explored, or they bring objects to the baby. Finally, when they respond to a baby's bids for social interaction, they tend to stimulate and arouse and engage the infant in affectionate social play. Caregivers use a more complex set of signals and responses for toddlers than they do for young infants.

on baby (see Bornstein, 1989). Keeping this breakdown in mind while caring for infants can also help you read their signals and understand the effect of your responses.

What Are Some Typical Characteristics of Responsiveness?

Some people are very responsive to children, some are moderately so, and some seldom respond. For example, in one study with infants only five months of age, some caregivers were found to be responsive during less than 5 percent of the time they were observed, whereas others were responsive during as much as 75 percent of the time. Surprisingly, this variation is true of individuals in the same social class and with approximately the same number of years in school (Bornstein and Tamis-LeMonda, 1989).

The nature of a caregiver's response typically varies with the age of the child and the type of children's activity the caregiver is responding to. A caregiver's initial response to a young baby's distress

How Does Responsiveness Affect a Baby's Expression of Distress?

Because crying is probably the most prominent signal that a baby is capable of producing initially, the frequency and manner in which caregivers should respond to cries have historically been of uppermost concern to them. Before responsiveness from caregivers became a subject of research studies, it was commonly believed that caregivers who responded too quickly to a child's cries would reinforce crying, and the child would learn to cry more often. Some 20 years ago Mary Salter Ainsworth and Silvia Bell of Johns Hopkins University decided to see whether this commonly held belief was true (Bell and Ainsworth, 1972). They periodically observed a group of mothers naturally interacting with their babies during the first year of life. At the conclusion of the study, Bell and Ainsworth found that the toddlers whose mothers had responded more often to their cries as babies actually cried less often, not more.

One possible explanation for this unexpected result was that when caregivers responded to children's signals, the children learned that they were not helpless but rather that their behaviors had an effect on the world. They could control their environment in a predictable and reliable way. Bell and Ainsworth hypothesized that, as the infants matured, they learned to substitute more sophisticated means of communicating for crying; hence they cried less than children whose caregivers did not impart this sense of control. Indeed, Bell and Ainsworth found that by the end of a child's first year, children of responsive parents not only cried less but their noncry communications were more varied, subtle, and clear. These children communicated using facial expressions, gesturing, and nondistress vocalization.

Bell and Ainsworth concluded that maternal responsiveness to infants' signals promotes a feeling of competence and confidence in children that fosters the development of communication and encourages the later development of a variety of cognitive skills. Indeed, evidence has been accumulating over the last two decades to support the hypothesis that babies whose caregivers respond to them may be at an advantage in a host of ways; for example, in learning, exploratory behavior, and motivation to learn. Responsiveness from caregivers may also benefit the social and emotional development of infants. These issues will be examined in the next sections.

How Does "Being Responsive" Affect Cognitive Development?

Michael Lewis and Susan Goldberg were among the first researchers to notice a positive relation between responsive caregiving and better cognitive performance in children (Lewis and Goldberg, 1969). They found that three-month-old babies whose mothers responded more frequently to their cries and vocalizations tended to learn about something new by looking at it more quickly than did children of less responsive mothers. Following the report of these findings in 1969, subsequent research studies have indicated that maternal responsiveness is frequently positively associated with children's cognitive performance.

For example, with Margaret Ruddy and Catherine Tamis-LeMonda, Marc Bornstein studied responsiveness in middle-class mothers of normal babies from New York City and its suburbs (Bornstein and Tamis-LeMonda, 1989). He discovered that responsiveness has short-term and long-term cognitive benefits for babies. One group of infants had mothers who, during the middle of the child's first year, were responsive to their child's nondistress signals (such as vocalization, facial expression, and movements). At thirteen months those infants tended to show an advantage in language and play. A second group consisted of four-year-old children whose mothers had been responsive when the children were infants. Those children tended to solve problems more efficiently and scored higher on a standardized intelligence test than did their peers with less responsive mothers.

Leila Beckwith, Sarale Cohen, and their colleagues at the University of California, Los Angeles, studied responsiveness in caregivers of at-risk preterm infants and found similar positive effects (Beckwith and others, 1976). They learned that infants who were more skillful at nine months in sensorimotor tasks (such as searching for a hidden object, using one object as a means to obtain another, or inventing a solution to a problem) had at one month of age experienced more mutual caregiver-infant gazing (that is, looking intently at one another); at three months, more interchanges of smiling during mutual gazing and more responsiveness to their cries; and at eight months, greater levels of social interaction, including more responsiveness to their nondistress vocalizations.

What is more, responsiveness may exert similar effects across different cultures. Bornstein and Tamis-LeMonda, with a Japanese colleague, Kazuo Miyake, conducted a study of children aged two and one-half years old in Sapporo, Japan. Their findings show that children whose mothers were responsive to them when they were four- to-five-month-old infants scored higher on a standardized mental achievement test than did children with less responsive mothers (Bornstein and Tamis-LeMonda, 1989).

Caregivers' responsiveness to nondistress vocalization seems to be particularly significant to the infant's development of language. For example, Leon Yarrow of the National Institutes of Health observed caregivers and their infants interacting at home. He noticed that, when caregivers provided contingent responsiveness to the vocalizations of an infant, that child tended to vocalize more fluently to a toy subsequently presented than did peers with less responsive caregivers (Yarrow and others, 1972). (*Contingent responsiveness* means that the caregiver responds only after the baby has vocalized.)

Kathleen Bloom and her colleagues at Dalhousie University, in Halifax, Nova Scotia, found that responsiveness helps to instill conversational rhythm in babies. When an adult experimenter responded contingently to three-month-old infants' vocalizations and maintained a turn-taking or speak-listen pattern throughout an experimental observation, babies as well tended to pause between vocalizations (Bloom, Russell, and Wassenberg, 1987). These babies also tended to produce a greater proportion of speech-like sounds than did a group of babies whose sounds received noncontingent responses.

As evidence of the long-term effects of being responsive to vocalizations, Beckwith and Cohen (1989) studied mothers of preterm children. Those mothers who were more verbally resposive to the children's nondistress vocalizations when the children were eight months and twenty-four months old had children who tended to have higher IQ scores at twelve years of age.

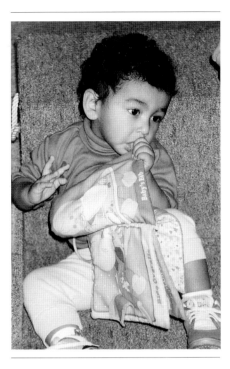 

Of course, many people had suspected for some time (mostly on account of studies of infants reared in institutions) that children deprived of social responsiveness normally fare poorly in development; but factors apart from responsiveness were also thought to enter into the poor prognosis for these children. Such babies tend to be undernourished and understimulated too. However, a study performed by Craig Ramey of the Frank Porter Graham Child Development Center at the University of North Carolina suggested that responsiveness is a significant factor in and of itself. He gave one group of failure-to-thrive infants a nutritional supplement and a comparable group the same nutritional supplement plus weekly responsive stimulation. The second group subsequently performed better than the first group on a learning task (Ramey and others, 1975). On this basis Ramey suggested that the quality of both nutrition and social responsiveness can reduce the effects of developmental retardation.

Ramey noticed something else intriguing about the children in the study: they showed a marked change in their social and emotional demeanor. Instead of being apathetic, they appeared alert and responsive themselves. Ramey could only speculate on the cause, but he suspected that responsive stimulation played a part. Since that time numerous studies have shown that being responsive to a child has a positive effect on the child's social and emotional life, an action that in turn can create a better environment for the child's cognitive development.

How Does Responsiveness in Infancy Alter Growth?

Research studies have shown that the experience of responsiveness can exert beneficial effects in development, but not always how it does so. On this aspect researchers are more tentative and speculative. But, as seen from discussions in previous sections, several possible mechanisms exist by which responsiveness might make its mark:

1. Responsiveness could instill feelings of control and power; that is, children learn that they have a positive effect on their environment. This discovery, in turn, might increase children's motivation to learn and their confidence in successfully solving problems. One study showed that infants, who had prior experience with stimulation they could control, learned more competently and efficiently in new situations than did infants who had prior experience with stimulation they could not control.

2. Responsive caregiving could promote self-regulation in children that facilitates attention and learning.

3. Responsive caregiving could simply provide caregivers and children with closely shared opportunities to learn about one another and thereby assist learning.

4. Responsiveness could elevate a child's mood, making the child feel more amenable to learning.

5. Last but by no means least, responsiveness may promote caregiver-infant attachment, which in turn determines the degree to which the infant feels secure to explore and learn about his or her world.

Where Does Responsiveness Come From?

Given the important role that responsiveness seems to play in development, one might reasonably ask how responsiveness arises in caregivers. Some believe that responsiveness represents purely biological functioning; others, that responsiveness develops out of experience. Some believe that women are naturally more responsive than men; others, that responsiveness is a trait that all members of the human community share—men, women, and children alike.

The Nobel Prize-winning ethologist Konrad Lorenz hypothesized that responsiveness is an unlearned instinct in adults, one that is deeply embedded in the psyche and automatically excited by key physical features of the infant, such as a large head in relation to the size of the rest of the body, a bulbous forehead, soft elastic skin, and the cry. Lorenz contended that those traits spontaneously and involuntarily "release" inborn emotional and motor reactions in adults. Indeed, that is why, Lorenz asserted, human beings feel so strongly not only about human babies but about animal babies in general, because the young of many species share the same basic "babyishness" attributes.

This theory notwithstanding, we know that caregivers in the same culture and from different cultures vary in the degree to which they are responsive. Indeed, some caregivers are abusive to their children. What accounts for these differences?

To date, little evidence exists that hormones play a significant role in the expression of human responsiveness (although future research may prove otherwise). Factors that play a role include characteristics of the caregiver (for example, an empathic and adaptable individual may be a more responsive caregiver); the circumstances under which the caregiver is functioning (for example, a caregiver with just a few children in his or her care may be able to be more responsive than a caregiver with many); and characteristics of the child (for example, a child who is irritable and difficult to soothe may temper his or her caregiver's responsiveness).

Although the variables are multiple, one variable has consistently been found to have an effect on the expression of human responsiveness—it is experience with children. For example, Mechthild Papoušek of the University of Munich, Germany, found that the amount of experience a caregiver had with infants or children prominently determined the degree of responsiveness to an infant's noncry vocalizations. In her study nonparent speech therapists and experienced parents were significantly better at reading two-month-olds' nondistress signals than were first-time parents (Papoušek, 1988).

Accumulating experience with a particular child seems to make a difference too. In one study a group of mothers watched an assessment scale for newborns being administered to their infants, received an explanation of the scale, and learned about their infants' performance on it. Later, mothers in this group showed significantly enhanced responsiveness while interacting with their infants as compared to a control group who had simply learned about children's toys and furnishings. An important finding revealed that the increased responsiveness of mothers who learned about the assessment of their infants was also reflected in the infants' own responsiveness (Anderson and Sawin, 1983). The babies whose mothers had learned about their babies' behavior showed a qualitative gain in alertness, positive affect and mood, and visual responsiveness to their mothers. Getting to know children can help caregivers to become more attuned to their children's needs, knowledge that in turn apparently leads to more alert and responsive children.

How Can You Become a More Responsive Caregiver?

To become responsive, you must be able to perceive an infant's signals; understand their meaning; and then respond contingently, appropriately, and promptly. The first step, perceiving, is straightforward. You have to be available and attentive. You should also know something about what you are looking and listening for. To some degree this knowledge comes with experience. Also, reading books on child development and how to care for children can be helpful. Interpreting what you perceive is a little harder. Is the baby crying because he or she is hungry, is overstimulated, or needs to be held? Finding the answer to this question comes not just from learning about babies generally but from learning about the particular baby you are caring for. Each child comes to the setting with his or her own temperament, daily rhythm, likes, and dislikes. By carefully watching the child, over time and in different contexts, a caregiver can understand that child's personality and will then be able to decipher that child's messages.

The final step, being able to respond contingently, appropriately, and promptly, is just an extension of understanding what the child needs. Once you understand the message, the response should follow suit. If a child looks at you with a big, broad smile, he or she probably would like you to smile back and maybe engage in social play. If the child then changes mood and starts to avert your gaze, he or she is probably saying, "I'm tired; I think I've had enough for now," and would like you to provide some quiet time. A toddler who moves from object to object with his of her index finger out, glancing over to you, probably wants you to give the word for each item. And when the toddler looks at you and says "Ba," the child probably would like you to look at him or her and say "Ba" back. A toddler who points to a ball and says "Ba" might like it if you said, "Yes, it's a ball. See how high it bounces." As you get to know each child, you learn to fine-tune your response. For some children social interaction might call for tickling or other rough-and-tumble play; other children might prefer

verbal games in response. If you are attentive and receptive to children's signals, children themselves will tell you much about what they need and want: when they would like stimulation and when they do not, when they need to be held and when they want the freedom to explore, when they are happy, and when they are sad. The more you can communicate to children that you have heard their message and that you understand, the more responsive you will be.

What Has Been Learned About Responsiveness from Research?

Findings from many research reports converge in showing the powerful role that responsiveness plays over the development of a broad range of children's competencies. Whether babies act or do not, their caregivers display the contingent, appropriate, and prompt reactions typically associated with responsiveness. To provide this kind of responsiveness, caregivers need to know each child in their care through developing a close relationship and being attentive and receptive to each child's signals. Responsiveness is a deceptively uncomplicated scenario. Hidden, however, are the telling

and powerful consequences responsiveness portends—not only for the infant's survival but also for the child's positive development of intellectual capability and social self-confidence.

References

Anderson, C. J., and D. B. Sawin. (1983). Enhancing responsiveness in mother-infant interaction. *Infant Behavior and Development,* 6, 361–68.

Beckwith, Leila, and others. (1989). Maternal responsiveness with preterm infants and competency at age twelve years. In *Maternal responsiveness: Characteristics and consequences.* Edited by M. H. Bornstein. Indianapolis: Wiley Publishers, pp. 75–87.

Beckwith, Leila, and others. (1976). Caregiver-infant interaction and early cognitive development in preterm infants. *Child Development,* Vol. 47, No. 3 (September), 579–87.

Bell, Sylvia M., and M. D. Ainsworth. (1972). Infant crying and maternal responsiveness. *Child Development,* Vol. 43, No. 4 (December), 1171–90.

Bloom, Kathleen; A. Russell; and K. Wassenberg. (1987). Turn taking affects the quality of infant vocalizations. *Journal of Child Language,* 14, 211–27.

Bornstein, Marc H., ed. (1989). *Maternal responsiveness: Characteristics and consequences.* San Francisco: Jossey-Bass, Inc., Publishers.

Bornstein, Marc H., and C. S. Tamis-LeMonda. (1989). Maternal responsiveness and cognitive development in children. In *Maternal responsiveness: Characteristics and consequences.* Edited by Marc H. Bornstein. San Francisco: Jossey-Bass, Inc., Publishers, pp. 49–61.

Lewis, Michael, and S. Goldberg. (1969). Perceptual-cognitive development in infancy: A generalized expectancy model as a function of the mother-infant interaction. *Merrill-Palmer Quarterly,* 15, 81–100.

Papoušek, M. (1988). *Determinants of responsiveness to infant vocal expression of emotional state.* Poster presented at the Sixth Biennial International Conference on Infant Studies, Washington, D.C.

Ramey, C. T., and others. (1975). Nutrition, response-contingent stimulation, and the maternal deprivation syndrome: Results of an early intervention program. *Merrill-Palmer Quarterly,* Vol. 21, No. 1 (January), 45–53.

Yarrow, Leon J., and others. (1972). Dimensions of early stimulation and their differential effects on infant development. *Merrill-Palmer Quarterly,* 18, 205–18.

Note: In support of this article, this addendum provides additional materials that have been published since the original publication of the guide.

Beckwith, Leila and others. (1993). Preterm children at early adolescence and continuity and discontinuity in maternal responsiveness from infancy. *Child Development,* Vol. 63 (March), 1198–1208.

Edwards, Carolyn P., and Helen H. Raikes. (2002). Extending the dance: relationship-based approaches to infant/toddler care and education. *Young Children,* Vol. 57 (July), 10–17.

Rofrano, Frances (2002). I care for you: A reflection on caring as infant curriculum. *Young Children,* Vol. 57 (January), 49–51.

Supporting Cognitive Development Through Interactions with Young Infants

Tiffany Field

Very young infants (from birth to six months of age) are fascinated by the world around them. They notice sights, sounds, smells, touches, and movements. When something catches their attention, they often want to find out more about it. If something happens once, they often enjoy seeing or hearing it happen again. Of greatest interest to them   what they want to learn most about—is their adult caregivers. Young infants focus intently on the actions of their caregivers. Facial expressions, smiles, sounds, touches, and gestures from the caregiver often delight them. Through innate responses such as smiles, coos, and raised eyebrows, young infants communicate what interests them

to their caregiver. Through playful exchanges of such behaviors as coos, facial expressions, and smiles with an adult who understands their messages, they learn how to take turns and how to interact with a partner.

The intellectual development of young infants depends on their ability to organize their behavior for interaction with their caregivers. To help young infants organize their behavior, caregivers need to know how to determine when young infants are ready to interact and learn from social exchanges and how to adjust to each child's individual rhythm and style during interaction. This chapter begins with an overview of the importance of the young infants' social behaviors and biological

rhythms in their development. The second part of the chapter will focus on responses and actions from the caregiver that enable very young infants to learn from social interaction.

Early Behaviors and Interaction

The young infant is capable of communicating to the caregiver through a host of signals. The primary means through which the infant communicates are looking behavior, facial expressions, vocalizations, and body movements.

Looking Behavior

During the early months of infancy, the primary skill of infants is looking behavior. Young infants can look at a person or thing, look away, close their eyes, and turn their heads. Looking behavior is the only system over which infants have a considerable degree of control and the only system that can be turned on or off. Caregivers spend virtually all of their one-to-one interaction time looking at the infant (Stern, 1974). However, whether the infant looks at the caregiver's face seems to depend on the infant's state of alertness and the type of stimulation the caregiver is providing (Field, 1977 a). The young infant seems to look away from the caregiver's face to process the stimulation he or she is receiving.

Because the infant can use visual behavior to tune in and out of a variety of stimulation, the infant's gazing (both looking at and looking away from the caregiver) becomes an important signal to the caregiver. The caregiver's reactions to an infant's gazing appear to play a critical role in engaging the infant in eye-to-eye contact. Consequently, T. Berry Brazelton and others have suggested that one of the most important skills for the caregiver to learn is sensitivity to the infant's capacity for attention and inattention (Brazelton,

Koslowski, and Main, 1974). Being sensitive to a young baby's looking behavior means stopping stimulating activity (touches, smiles, coos, and so forth) when the infant becomes inattentive or looks away. In effect, the infant is saying, "For right now, I've had enough cooing, smiling, laughing, and tickling. Give me some time to settle down." After a while, if the baby calms down and looks at you with bright eyes, he or she is saying, "I am ready for some action. Let's be playful."

Thus, gaze alternation, or looking at and looking away, is natural behavior that is affected by the type, amount, and timing of stimulation (Stern, 1974). The infant (like the adult) needs periods of looking away to process the stimulation he or she received during the previous looking period or simply to calm down (Field, 1981). When the adult fails to respect the infant's looking-away periods and interprets them as the infant's needing a break from the conversation, the interaction becomes difficult or disturbed (Brazelton, Koslowski, and Main, 1974; Field, 1977 a). With too much stimulation and no chance to settle down, a young baby can easily become over-excited and perhaps fussy. In such a state the infant is no longer able to interact in an organized way.

Although alternating looking at and looking away from the caregiver is typical behavior for young infants, some infants, at a very early stage, persistently avert their gaze (always look away) even with sensitive caregivers. In some cases such avoidant behavior may be due to the infant's temperament. Some infants may react strongly to bright lights, noise, or touch; and as a result, these infants may avoid stimulation from caregivers. In addition, caregivers may have difficulty interacting with infants whose innate temperaments are characterized by low levels of alertness, cuddliness, consolability, and visual attentiveness. The chapter by Stella Chess, "Temperaments of Infants and Toddlers," in *Infant/Toddler Caregiving: A Guide to Social-Emotional Growth and Socialization* and the video, *Flexible, Fearful, or Feisty: The Temperaments of Infants and Toddlers,* provide more detailed information on temperament and its effects on interactions with infants. (See Section Five.)

Face, Voice, and Body

Infants' smiling and laughter are behaviors that delight caregivers. During early interactions such behaviors seldom occur spontaneously except when they are elicited by tickling or game playing (Sroufe and Wunsch, 1972). A facial expression that occurs relatively often is the raised eyebrow, a kind of curiosity expression. The infant's pout-and-cry faces are very familiar to caregivers. Because these expressions often look quite adult-like, they are easy to interpret as signals of discontent. Pout-and-cry faces typically signal the end of a face-to-

face interaction. Similarly, crying, arching of the back, and general squirming typically precede the end of an interaction. Sometimes this pattern means that the infant is simply tired; sometimes, that the caregiver is overstimulating the child; and sometimes, that the infant is simply uncomfortable in the face-to-face position.

Activity Rhythms and Interaction

The very young infant's biological rhythms influence when the child is ready to interact with an adult; for example, from being awake to falling asleep, from being active to becoming inactive, and from being attentive to becoming inattentive. When preparing for interaction, the caregiver needs to give special attention to two aspects of biological rhythms: namely, the young infant's state of alertness and pauses in activity.

State of Alertness

An infant interacts best with a caregiver when the infant is awake and alert. At the beginning the young infant moves from a sleeping state to an awake state frequently and stays awake for only short periods of time. During the next several weeks and months, the young infant becomes increasingly organized so that most of the sleep time is consolidated at nighttime and periods of alertness become longer. The increasingly longer sleep-awake cycle is a biological rhythm consisting of several phases. Infants who are awake experience fluctuating periods of alertness; and within periods of alertness, infants become attentive and inattentive. If the caregiver interacts with an infant who is awake but not fully alert or ready for interaction, the infant will often try to avoid the stimulation from the caregiver; or the infant may quickly become inattentive or even fussy. In contrast, by waiting for an optimal state

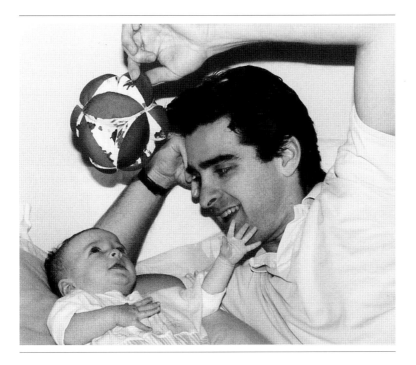

of alertness, the caregiver can help the infant sustain attention or moments of alertness for interaction.

In general, as the infant learns to organize his or her various activity rhythms (for example, sucking, gaze alternations, and limb movements), interactions can become more prolonged. Caregivers can facilitate this development by being sensitive and adapting to the infant's rhythms and other signals of interaction and thereby support a rhythmical turn-taking interaction.

Pauses in Activity

Biological rhythms become more stabilized during the first few months; for example, sleep-awake periods become more prolonged (Thoman, 1975). Yet infants and adults continue to have to adjust to each other's rhythms. An example of this process of adjustment comes from a study of interactions between a caregiver and an infant during bottle-feeding. Adult stimulation was found to be typically reserved for pauses in the sucking activity or for times when the infant could interact freely because he or she was not preoccupied with sucking (Field, 1977 b).

Role of the Adult Partner

The caregiver's role in early learning is both multifaceted and quite special. Designing, maintaining, and changing the environment; keeping the daily schedule and the environment organized; and providing interesting stimulation are large tasks in themselves. On top of that the caregiver needs to be a sensitive, responsive interaction partner who offers a variety of interesting games to the infant. Face-to-face interaction is extremely critical to the overall development of the very young infant, including the learning of early social skills, such as facial expressions and turn-taking.

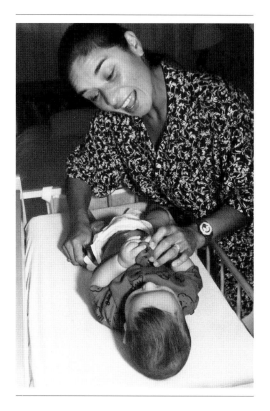

Face-to-face interaction can take place when the infant is on the caregiver's lap, in an infant seat, or lying on his or her back on the floor. In any of these situations, the head of the caregiver should be lined up approximately with that of the infant at about 15 inches from the infant's face so that the infant can clearly see the caregiver's face. Being placed in a face-to-face position with the caregiver is typically popular with infants for at least the first eight months of life. After that time the infant becomes more interested in manipulating objects and moving around while learning to crawl.

Simplifying Behavior

Behaviors of adult caregivers are of course much more developed than the infant's. Much of what the caregiver needs to do has been described as "infantized" behavior (Field, 1978).

Ways to simplify or infantize behavior include slowing down and exaggerating speech in a manner referred to as baby talk or motherese (Stern, 1974). Facial expressions are also exaggerated, slowed down, and prolonged. When a caregiver interacts with a young infant, the slowing down of speech and exaggeration of facial expressions help the infant process or understand the caregiver's behaviors. Thus, when a caregiver infantizes behavior during interaction, the infant is more able to follow what the caregiver is doing and become more effective at turn taking.

Responding Contingently

As described by Bornstein and Bornstein elsewhere in this guide, contingent responses occur within seconds of the infant's behavior and either meet the infant's communicated need or are similar to the infant's behavior. Several researchers have suggested that contingent or prompt responses similar to the infant's action are necessary so that the infant can feel that he or she has some influence on the interaction (Ainsworth and Bell, 1974; Goldberg, 1977; Lewis and Goldberg, 1969; Watson, 1967). If the caregiver's response is appropriate and occurs within a few seconds of the infant's behavior, the infant will more likely perceive that the caregiver's behavior is a direct response to his or her own behavior. Research studies have shown that adults view infant behaviors such as smiling, cooing, and eye-to-eye contact as positive responses. Such responses encourage adults to continue the game. For example, infants' smiling and vocalizing are frequently followed by similar behaviors from adults (Gewirtz and Gewirtz, 1969; Lewis and Wilson, 1972).

Imitating

Research studies have shown that a lot of caregiving behavior is imitative. Adults probably imitate the infant's behavior so that the infant may more easily understand his or her own behavior.

Infants enjoy being imitated and are more able to imitate caregiver's imitations of their own behaviors (Field, Guy, and Umbel, 1985). Thus, when interacting in a one-to-one situation with an infant, caregivers typically imitate the most frequently occurring infant behaviors; for example, grimaces more than laughter in the very young infant and laughter more than grimaces in the slightly older infant. Very soon after birth, infants are able to imitate simple behaviors such as sticking their tongues out and making happy, sad, and surprised faces (Field and others, 1982; Meltzoff and Moore, 1977).

Repeating Behavior

Repetition of actions is another way to help infants understand the interaction partner more easily. Repetition gives the infant multiple opportunities to connect his or her actions with those of the adult.

Highlighting

A frequently occurring behavior of caregivers is called "highlighting" of the infant's behaviors. Caregivers frequently give a running commentary or verbally describe and label the infant's behaviors as they happen. For example, if the infant has hiccups, the caregiver will say, "Oh, you have the hiccups" or "Sweet baby, you always spit up when you get happy."

Playing Games

Caregivers also play a number of games that have been observed around the world and labeled infant games. They include "peek-a-boo," "so big," "tell me a

story," "crawling," "itsy-bitsy spider," and "pat-a-cake" (Field, 1979). These games invariably lead to smiling and laughter from the infant but should be played when the child is at the appropriate age. When a caregiver tries to play age-inappropriate games (for example, playing "pat-a-cake" with a six-week-old rather than with a three-month-old infant), the interaction will be disrupted. A six-week-old infant will be unable to follow a game like "pat-a-cake" and may become upset or inattentive if the caregiver initiates such a game. In contrast, the typical three-month-old infant will be able to follow the caregiver's movements during "pat-a-cake" and will usually remain attentive and enjoy the game. Being sensitive to the baby's signals will help the caregiver to know whether a game is appropriate or inappropriate for an infant.

Infants' games also provide opportunities for turn taking or responsive give-and-take with an infant. One of the most popular games of the young infant is "tell me a story." The words are provided by

the caregiver, who treats the infant's vocalizations as if they, too, are words. For instance, in playing the game, the caregiver asks, "Do you want to tell me a story?" the infant coos; the adult responds, "Oh yeah? and then what happened?" The infant coos again, and the adult replies, "Oh, that's funny." The infant smiles, coos, and sometimes laughs; and the caregiver then responds by playing more of the same game. When the infant no longer responds contentedly to the game, that is a signal to move on to still another game or "conversation" or perhaps to give the child a chance to become organized for more interaction, have private time, or take a rest.

Summary

The very young infant's development in general and intellectual development in particular depend on the presence of a caregiver who:

- Waits until the infant is in a quiet, attentive state of alertness before interacting with the infant
- Responds promptly when the child expresses an interest or need
- "Infantizes" or slows down, exaggerates, and repeats behaviors
- Responds by imitating or highlighting the infant's behaviors
- Takes turns and does not interrupt the infant
- Plays games that are interesting and age appropriate
- Respects the infant's occasional breaks from the interaction

Becoming a sensitive interaction partner makes caregiving fun because the infant enjoys and appreciates such care. At the same time sensitive and responsive caregiving provides the infant with the experiences he or she needs to understand and learn about the world.

References

Ainsworth, M. D. S., and S. M. Bell. (1974). Mother-infant interaction and the development of competence. In *The growth of competence*. Edited by K. J. Connolly and J. S. Bruner. New York: Academic Press, Inc.

Brazelton, T. B.; B. Koslowski; and M. Main. (1974). The origins of reciprocity: The early mother-infant interaction. In *The effect of the infant on its caregiver*. Edited by M. Lewis and L. Rosenblum. New York: John Wiley and Sons, Inc.

Field, T. (1977 a). Effects of early separation, interactive deficits, and experimental manipulations on infant-mother face-to-face interaction. *Child Development,* Vol. 48, No. 3 (September), 763–71.

Field, Tiffany M. (1977 b). Maternal stimulation during infant feeding. *Developmental Psychology,* Vol. 13, No. 5 (September), 539–40.

Field, Tiffany M. (1978). The three Rs of infant-adult interactions: Rhythms, repertoires, and responsivity. *Journal of Pediatric Psychology,* 3, 131–36.

Field, Tiffany M. (1979). Games parents play with normal and high-risk infants. *Child Psychiatry and Human Development,* 10, 41–48.

Field, Tiffany M. (1981). Gaze behavior of normal and high-risk infants during early interactions. *Journals of the American Academy of Child Psychiatry,* 20, 308–17.

Field, Tiffany M., and others. (1982). Discrimination and imitation of facial expressions by neonates. *Science,* Vol. 218, No. 4568 (October 8), 179–81.

Field, Tiffany M.; L. Guy; and V. Umbel. (1985). Infants' responses to mothers' imitative behaviors. *Infants Mental Health Journal,* 6, 40–44.

Gewirtz, H. B., and J. L. Gewirtz. (1969). Caretaking settings, background events, and behavior differences in four Israeli child rearing environments: Some preliminary trends. In *Determinants of infant behavior.* Edited by B. Foss. Vol. 4. London: Methuen.

Goldberg, S. (1977). Social competence in infancy: A model of parent-infant interaction. *Merrill-Palmer Quarterly,* Vol. 23, No. 3 (July), 163–77.

Lewis, Michael, and S. Goldberg. (1969). Perceptual-cognitive development in infancy: A generalized expectancy model as a function of the mother-infant interaction. *Merrill-Palmer Quarterly,* Vol. 15, No. 1 (January), 81–100.

Lewis, Michael, and Cornelia D. Wilson. (1972). Infant development in lower-class American families. *Human Development,* 15, 112–27.

Meltzoff, Andrew N., and M. K. Moore. (1977). Imitation of facial and manual gestures by human neonates. *Science,* Vol. 198, No. 4312 (October 7), 75–78.

Sroufe, L. A., and J. P. Wunsch. (1972). The development of laughter in the first year of life. *Child Development,* Vol. 43, No. 4 (December), 1326–44.

Stern, D. N. (1974). Mother and infant at play: The dyadic interaction involving facial, vocal, and gaze behaviors. In *The effect of the infant on its caregiver.* Edited by M. Lewis and L. A. Rosenblum. New York: John Wiley and Sons, Inc.

Thoman, E. B. (1975). Early development of sleeping behaviors in infants. In *Studies in mother-infant interaction.* Edited by H. R. Schaffer. London: Academic Press, Inc.

Watson, J. S. (1967). Memory and "contingency analysis" in infant learning. *Merrill-Palmer Quarterly,* 13, 55–76.

Note: In support of this article, this addendum provides additional materials that have been published since the original publication of the guide.

Pratt, Martha W. (1999). The importance of infant/toddler interactions." *Young Children,* Vol. 54 (July), 26–29.

Suizzo, Marie-Anne. (2002). The social-emotional and cultural contexts of cognitive development: Neo-Piagetian perspectives. *Child Development,* Vol. 71 (July/August), 846–49.

Caregivers' Practices That Support Cognitive Development

The visions listed here are excerpts from Vision VII in *Visions for Infant/Toddler Care: Guidelines for Professional Caregiving.* Sacramento: California Department of Education, 1988, pp. 35–36. (See also page 2 in this guide, "Cognitive Development: Vision Statement.")

Vision: Exploring and trying to understand the world are natural and necessary for children's cognitive or intellectual development. As children learn and grow, their thinking capacities expand and become more flexible. Adults should support and guide this process by responding to children's interests with new learning opportunities and to their questions with information and enthusiasm. Cognitive growth also requires healthy development in other areas: physical growth and development of motor skills, a secure emotional base, and positive social interactions.

Practices: The infant/toddler caregiver working in *a center or family day care home:*

- Observes children's play frequently to assess their cognitive development and readiness for new learning opportunities
- Uses techniques and activities that stimulate children's curiosity, inventiveness, and problem-solving and communication skills
- Gives children time and space for extended concentrated play and adjusts routines and schedules for this purpose
- Provides opportunities for children to try out and begin to understand the relationships between cause and effect and means and ends
- Understands the importance of play, shows genuine interest, and often joins children's play as a partner and facilitator
- Uses the center or home environment, everyday activities, and homemade materials to encourage children's intellectual development
- Helps children discover ways to solve problems that arise in daily activities
- Supports children's repetitions of the familiar and introduces new experiences, activities, and materials when children are interested and ready
- Recognizes differences in individual learning styles and finds ways to work effectively with each child
- Encourages child-initiated activities and active learning rather than adult talking and children's passive listening
- Obtains (or makes) and uses special learning materials and equipment for children whose handicaps affect their ability to learn
- Provides equipment and materials that children can explore and master by themselves

- Is alert to the task a child is attempting and provides appropriate support
- Recognizes learning problems and makes referrals according to the policy of the center or program

Vision: *Young infants* (birth to nine months) begin cognitive or intellectual learning through their interactions with playful, caring adults in a secure environment. Some of their early learning includes becoming familiar with distance and space relationships, sounds, similarities, and differences among things, and visual perspectives from various positions (front, back, under, and over). Such learning can be reinforced by describing to infants what they feel, hear, touch, and see.

Practices: The caregiver working with *young infants* also, for example:
- Talks to infants, describing what they feel, hear, touch, and see
- Encourages manipulation and inspection of a variety of objects
- Provides opportunities for infants to interact with adults and children and watch interactions of adults and children
- Encourages infants in imitating others
- Plays with infants frequently

Vision: *Mobile infants* (six to eighteen months) actively learn through trying things out; using objects as tools; comparing; imitating; looking for lost objects; and naming familiar objects, places, and people. By giving the infants opportunities to explore space, objects, and people and by sharing children's pleasure in discovery, adults can help children become confident in their ability to learn and understand.

Practices: The caregiver working with *mobile infants* also, for example:
- Talks, sings, plays with, and reads to mobile infants
- Gives children more space to explore as they become more mobile
- Gives children many opportunities to figure out cause and effect, how things work
- Provides many experiences with moving, hiding, and changing objects

Vision: *Toddlers* (sixteen to thirty-six months) enter into a new and expansive phase of mental activity. They are beginning to think in words and symbols, to remember, and to imagine. Their curiosity leads them to try out materials in many ways. Adults can encourage this natural interest by providing a variety of new, open-ended materials for experimentation. They can create a supportive social environment for learning by showing enthusiasm for the children's individual discoveries; encouraging them to name things and talk about their experiences and observations; asking questions that have more than one answer; and encouraging the children to compare and contrast objects, sensations, and events.

Practices: The caregiver working with *toddlers* also, for example:

- Encourages children to ask questions and seek help and responds to them in ways that extend their thinking; for example, "That's a good question; let's see if we can find out."
- Asks questions that have more than one answer, encouraging children to wonder, guess, and talk about their ideas; for example, "What do you think might happen?" or "How do you feel when . . . ?"
- Encourages children to name objects and to talk about their experiences and observations
- Provides opportunities to organize and form groups and to compare and contrast thoughts, words, objects, and sensations
- Involves toddlers in projects such as cooking, gardening, and repairing, when possible
- Reduces distractions and interruptions so that toddlers have opportunities to extend their attention span and work on one activity, such as block building or water play, for a long period of time

Section Two:
Learning Environments

Learning Environments: Vision Statement

The caregiver uses space, relationships, materials, and routines as resources for constructing an interesting, secure, and enjoyable environment that encourages play, exploration, and learning.

Children of all ages learn through their own experiences, trial and error, repetition, and imitation. Adults can guide and encourage children's learning by ensuring that the environment is emotionally appropriate; invites play, active exploration, and movement by children; and supports a broad array of experiences. A reliable framework of routines, together with a stimulating choice of activities and materials, facilitates children's learning. Thoughtful caregivers recognize that the learning environment includes both people and relationships between people and that attention to the way in which environments are set up and used is an important contribution to the quality of a learning experience.

Young infants (birth to nine months) begin to learn from their immediate surroundings and daily experiences. The sense of well-being and emotional security conveyed by a loving and skilled caregiver creates a readiness for other experiences. Before infants can creep and crawl, caregivers should provide a variety of sensory experiences and encourage movement and playfulness.

Mobile infants (six to eighteen months) are active, independent, and curious. They are increasingly persistent and purposeful in doing things. They need many opportunities to practice new skills and explore the environment within safe boundaries. Adults can share children's delight in themselves, their skills, and discoveries and gradually add variety to the learning environment.

Toddlers (sixteen to thirty-six months) are developing new language skills, physical control, and awareness of themselves and others each day. They enjoy participation in planned and group activities, but they are not yet ready to sit still or work in a group for very long. Adults can support the toddlers' learning in all areas by maintaining an environment that is dependable but flexible enough to provide opportunities for them to extend their skills, understanding, and judgment in individual ways.

The Physical Environment and Its Role in Influencing the Development of Infants and Toddlers

Theodore D. Wachs

When experts in child development are asked to advise caregivers on how to facilitate the intellectual development of infants and toddlers, most of the advice centers on the *social environment*, particularly on how caregivers should relate to their children. While caregiver-infant relations have a critical influence on a child's development, they are not the only environmental influence (see the chapters by the Bornsteins and Field in this guide). The *physical environment* also plays an important role in the development of infants.

Perhaps the best way to understand what is meant by the *physical environment* is to think of the infant's world as if it were a movie in which "actors" (the child's parents or caregivers) read to the child, play with the child, and respond to the child's needs. These actors form the child's social environment. However, the movie (the infant's world) consists of more than just actors. It also takes place on a stage, which contains various props such as different types of toys, furniture, utensils, outside noises, or television programs. It is this *stage or setting on which children and caregivers relate to each other that defines what we mean by the physical environment.* While the physical environment of the infant usually involves nonliving things such as toys, people can also form part of the physical environment or stage when they are near

the child but are not likely to relate to the child. For example, if a caregiver is taking a small group of toddlers on a walk through a park, other people nearby can be considered part of the background set on which the children and caregiver are relating to each other.

The relationship between aspects of the physical environment and the infant's or toddler's intellectual development has been a neglected area of study for a long time. In part this neglect has occurred because many experts assumed that any effects of the physical environment on an infant's development were due to the infant's social environment. However, this assumption has been disproven by both animal and human research studies that have shown that the physical environment

can affect early development regardless of the nature of the social environment.

For example, in one study laboratory rats were raised in isolation, completely separated from other rats. Objects were put into the cages of some of the rats raised in isolation. Other rats, raised in similar conditions, had no objects in their cages. The brain development of the rats with objects in their cages turned out to be superior to that of the rats that did not have any objects in their cages. (Diamond, 1988).

For those of you who do not think that the study of rats reveals very much about what influences human children, my own research studies on the effects of environment on the development of infants and toddlers have repeatedly demonstrated that, even after we take into account all of the relevant relations between children and caregivers, specific aspects of the physical environment still influence the development of infants and toddlers (Wachs, 1986; Wachs, 1990). Not only does this research show that the physical environment directly influences the development of infants, but it also shows that specific aspects of the physical environment may influence how caregivers relate to their infants.

Similar findings have also come from research studies in other countries, results which indicate that aspects of the child's physical environment may also affect how the caregiver treats the child. For example, a study of caregiver practices on two Pacific islands

(Timor and New Guiana) showed that caregivers on Timor restricted their child's attempts to explore the environment (McSwain, 1981). The difference occurred because the villagers on Timor lived in rocky, hilly country, an environment that could cause serious injury to a child who freely explored it. With this type of physical setting, it is not at all surprising that caregivers restricted their child's attempts to explore the environment. Obviously, this example is dramatic; but as we shall see, a similar pattern occurs when we look at physical dimensions of child care environments.

The Influence of the Physical Environment

Given that the stage or setting in which children live can influence their development, what specific features of the physical environment are the most important?[1] Research studies have shown that some aspects of the physical environment are positive influences, helping infants and toddlers to become more competent. In contrast, other aspects are negative influences tending to inhibit or slow a child's intellectual development. Examples of both positive and negative influences of the physical environment follow.

Positive Influences of the Physical Environment

Features or aspects of the environment that support children's early development include the availability of toys and other objects, the variety of available toys and objects, the extent to which toys in the environment are appropriate for the age of the children, and the responsivity of objects in the environment.

1. *Availability of objects.* Does the sheer number of toys or objects available to the child influence development, or is development related more to the specific characteristics of available objects or toys? Research studies have shown that providing children with lots of toys and play objects does promote early intellectual competence, particularly for infants below nine months of age (Wachs and Gruen, 1982). Young

infants who are not mobile need a variety of toys within their reach. After the child becomes mobile, it may be more important to have plenty of less accessible toys in the environment (not within easy reaching distance) so that the child has to explore and learn about the environment while seeking a toy.

2. *Variety of toys or objects.* The term *variety,* when used in the context of objects and toys available to the infant, has two different meanings: The first one is *short-term variety,* which refers to the number of different objects or toys immediately available to the child. The second one is *long-term variety,* which refers to changes in the objects or toys available as the child develops. Having a number of different toys or play objects is initially important for the young child's development (short-term variety). However, if the types of toys or play objects the child has available (long-term variety) are not changed sufficiently, the initial benefits of short-term variety will be lost.

3. *The need to have objects that are appropriate for the child's level of development.* Many researchers believe that the development of infants is aided when they play with objects that offer new challenges or pose problems that are *slightly* more difficult than those offered by the children's current set of play objects. At the same time the toy or play object cannot be too complex. The infant cannot learn new things from play objects or toys that are too simple. The infant will not know how to use a complex toy or object

---

[1] For more information on the influence of the physical environment and for guidelines and practical suggestions on how to set up environments for infants and toddlers, see the document, *Infant/Toddler Caregiving: A Guide to Setting Up Environments,* and the video, *Space to Grow: Creating a Child Care Environment for Infants and Toddlers.* More information about these materials appears in Section Five. Also see the last page in this publication for information on ordering these materials.

meaningfully. Thus, whether an object or toy is too complex, too simple, or just right for a child depends on his or her age.

Another consideration is that objects often have *different uses when a child is at different ages*. In other words, a child can do one thing with an object at one age and use the same object differently at a later age. For example, a set of nested cups may be appropriate for young infants who explore the cups by chewing and fingering them. The

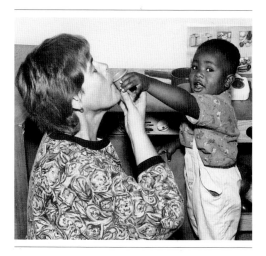

children will eventually become bored with the cups after they have explored and fingered them sufficiently. However, at a later age the children may again find the cups interesting to use for placing one cup inside of another as a means of learning about the size and properties of objects. Once the children have mastered this task, they will again lose interest in the cups. However, children's interest in the cups may rekindle as the children become older and get involved in pretend and fantasy play. Toddlers may use the cups to serve tea to dolls.

4. *Responsivity of objects.* We often think of people as being responsive to the child's actions, but we rarely think of objects in the same way. Yet, in fact, many toys or common objects can be highly responsive to the child's actions. What does *responsivity* mean? *Responsivity of objects means a change in an object's characteristics of sound or sight when the infant does something to an object.* For example, a small bell on a bootie is highly responsive for a very young infant because it makes a noise when the child kicks his or her foot. A spell-and-speak toy is an example of a responsive toy for an older child because when the child pulls the string, the toy emits animal sounds or a voice. In addition to toys, common household objects can also be responsive. For example, parents regard an infant's playing with the on/off sound-level controls of the television set as annoying. However, to the infant this device is a very responsive object, since small movements of the hand can turn the

picture on the television set on or off or can change soft sounds to loud (even deafening) ones. Researchers have consistently found that the more an infant is exposed to responsive objects, the more the infant's development advances (Wohlwill and Heft, 1987).

Having a variety of age-appropriate, responsive objects available is important for the development of infants and young children. Why is this so? Generally speaking, infants and young children spend a tremendous amount of time exploring the world around them. In fact, many American infant development specialists believe that infants and young children learn best through self-directed exploration. When a child explores objects, he or she develops an understanding of their differences (such as size, shape, and color), as well as of their uses. Under these conditions objects can serve as tools, helping the child to solve problems (for example, "I can't reach that little toy car by myself, but I can use this stick to help me get the toy car"). Similarly, objects can also serve as reference points, aiding the children in making finer distinctions about their world (for example, "Why does the square block go into the square hole and not into the round hole?").

When the child uses objects to solve problems or becomes involved with responsive objects, he or she is increasingly motivated to explore further and become involved with the environment. Children are rewarded when they succeed at getting objects to respond in certain ways, in using objects to solve

problems, or in solving problems posed by objects. The rewards are especially significant if the object is slightly different (variety) or slightly more difficult to use (age-appropriate) than are objects that the child has previously encountered. Thus, successfully dealing with a variety of age-appropriate, responsive objects not only helps the child learn something about problem solving but also motivates the child to do more with objects in the environment.

Negative Influences of the Physical Environment

Features or aspects of the environment that inhibit or negatively influence the development of infants and toddlers include physically restricted exploration, excessive background noise, and a crowded environment.

1. *Physically restricted exploration.* Because the infant's exploration is important, anything that interferes with it may also interfere with the infant's intellectual development. Some aspects of the physical environment can stop infants from exploring. For example, some objects can inhibit exploration such as playpens, gates (unless necessary for safety), and walkers (infants may be able to get around, but they cannot easily touch objects on the floor while they are in a walker). Less obvious aspects of the physical environment that can also inhibit exploration include shuttered or curtained windows that prevent the infant from looking outside the house. Of course, safety of the infant is critical; but within the requirements for safety, less physi-

cally restricted infants are more eager to explore.

2. *Excessive background noise.* Humans can tolerate only certain amounts of noise. If stimulation becomes excessive, adults often try to deal with it by tuning it out (filtering). For example, people who live near busy airports are often not as sensitive to the noise of planes taking off and landing as are people who do not live near airports. For infants and toddlers the danger is that in trying to filter out excess, unwanted stimulation, they may also filter out features of the environment that promote development. For example, research studies have shown that children who live in noisy conditions are less sensitive to language stimulation than are children who live in quiet surroundings. This decreased sensitivity is believed to occur because in filtering out the unwanted noise, the children are also tuning out adult speech sounds as well (Cohen and others, 1986).

Another factor is that infants and toddlers may be particularly susceptible to the negative effects of noise because they are physically less able to filter out noise or move away from it as easily as older children can. What caregivers often do not realize is the amount of unnecessary background noise that goes on in the child care setting. For example, in a family child care home, sufficient noise may be produced to inhibit the development of infants or toddlers in that setting. Sources of noise may include the television set, children banging toys or yelling at each other, or outside noises, such as those from trucks or cars passing on nearby streets.

3. *Crowded environments.* No one likes to be in crowded environments. Such surroundings make adults feel anxious or edgy. Being in crowded environments may also inhibit the intellectual development of infants and toddlers. Overcrowding may result from a low ratio in the number of activity areas to the number of

children in them. When a space is divided into only one or two areas, too many people may congregate in one area. In an environment with a low-activity-to-children ratio, a small number of activity areas are available to the infant or toddler and to a large number of children in the setting. Those conditions are not good for the development of infants.

Overcrowding may also be due to a lot of traffic in the child care environment. In this context *traffic* refers to the number of people coming and going through specific areas during the day. If a large number of people (parents and staff) are coming and going in the environment during the day, the impact on the children's development may be as detrimental as having a large number of children in one open room. Some areas in the child care environment should have a low amount of traffic and be as far away as possible from areas where traffic is necessary.

In general, crowding or some sources of noise like outside traffic are out of the child's control (remember what was said earlier about the importance of responsive environments). Children who are unable to control the level of excessive noise or crowding may develop learned helplessness. *Learned helplessness* means that even though children have the intellectual capacity to solve problems, they may not do so because they have learned, through experience, that their actions do not influence what goes on in their environment. Under such circumstances children may simply stop

trying, become passive, and not actively interact or try to learn from their environment.

Finally, recent research studies have suggested that the more noise or crowding in the environment, the less effective caregivers will be in relating to their children. For example, in noisy, crowded environments, caregivers typically are less involved with their children, vocalize less to them, and do fewer demonstrations of objects for them. Similarly, in noisy, crowded environments caregivers are less likely to be responsive to the child's vocalization or distress and more likely to interfere with the child's actions (Wachs, 1986). Thus, factors such as noise and crowding not only may directly hinder development, by causing the child to filter out unwanted noise or to develop a sense of learned helplessness but also may interfere with development by causing caregivers to behave inappropriately for the children's development.

Providing Appropriate Physical Environments

An understanding of the key features of the physical environment and of their influence on the intellectual development of infants and toddlers are concepts that can be used in the design and operation of group care settings. Specifically, what can be done to make the physical environment more appropriate for infants and toddlers? The section that follows provides some suggestions:

1. Provide a variety of play objects for the child. This does not mean giving the child lots and lots of play objects at once. You need to provide a

variety of objects for the child; however, you also need to know when to change play objects after the child has lost interest in the object. Obviously, changing objects becomes harder if the child is given everything at once.

When should play objects be changed? Knowing when to change play objects comes from watching the children. When given a new object, children tend to explore it actively at first. They may leave it for a while and then go back and play with it again. However, as the children become more familiar with the object's uses, they will play with it less. If a child is not using specific play objects for some period of time, that may be a signal to replace them with different ones. Thus, even if the setting has lots of toys, not all of them should be available at the same time. Some toys should be put away for a while and taken out later, rather than being put out all at once.

2. Provide a variety of available places for the child to get into, if at all possible. Try to arrange the area so that toddlers can choose their own preferred spaces to explore and play in. Having a variety of different spaces for children may be important in order to match the child's characteristics with those of the environment. Researchers have emphasized the importance of providing a variety of "defensible" spaces. This term refers to places where the child can observe group activities before deciding whether or not to join in. Partially enclosed space underneath a climbing structure, such as a wooden play bridge, would be an example of a defensible space. Defensible spaces may provide a particularly appropriate environment for a very shy child, who may need this type of space to observe what is going on in a noisy, active play situation before deciding whether or not to join in.

3. Be careful to note whether the objects in the environment are appropriate for the ages of the children. When selecting play objects, look for those with multiple uses across different age periods in addition to choosing objects that are appropriate primarily for a child at one age.

4. Make responsive objects available for the children. Providing these materials may be *particularly important* for group care settings, where by definition *children outnumber caregivers*. Because the chances are lower that the caregiver will respond quickly and appropriately to an individual child, the availability of objects that are responsive to the child may compensate for slower responses from caregivers. Thus, in providing play

child walks around the pull toy, it makes sounds.

5. Do not child-proof the environment to the point that exploration is inhibited. However, be sure to maintain essential standards of safety. This recommendation means, among other things, avoiding the use of playpens. Similarly, rather than locking a large number of cupboards and doors, you might put all dangerous objects in one or two cupboards or drawers and leave the rest available for the infants to explore.

objects for the child, look for ones that change in some way, either visually or with sound, as the child does things with the object (for example, wind-up toys).

Not all responsive objects have to be store-bought. Many examples exist of highly responsive objects that can be made by using simple materials. Sally McGregor, a pediatrician working in the West Indies, has developed inexpensively made, highly responsive sets of toys (McGregor, 1980). An example of such a toy for young infants is a rattle. To make the toy, the caregiver takes a small see-through plastic bottle, cuts slices of colored plastic from other bottles, puts the plastic slices into the see-through bottle, and seals the top. The child responds both visually and auditorially to the rattle. Cans with plastic tops can be used to make responsive toys for older children. For example, to make a pull toy, the caregiver punches a small hole in the plastic top, threads string through the hole, closes the hole by tying a knot inside, puts some bottle tops inside the can, and seals the top. As the

6. *Eliminate unnecessary noise* in a child care setting. For example, in a family child care home, the television set should be turned off if no one is watching it because this sound only adds to the level of background noise. The same point also applies to radios, tape decks, or

other sound equipment. This practice is particularly true if children are actively playing. Under those conditions no one will be able to hear the television set or radio, so turning them off will decrease unnecessary noise. *As a general rule it is probably appropriate to allow sound sources like television or audiotape to be turned on only on special occasions when a caregiver is available to watch or listen with the children.*

Obviously, in many caregiving environments completely escaping from noise or crowding is difficult, if not impossible. However, this situation does not mean that children have to be exposed to crowding or noise all the time. Dividing the space and making sure that only a small number of children occupy each area reduces crowding. Caregivers should provide a place or places where the child can go to be away from noise or people. This type of special place is called a "stimulus shelter."

How do caregivers provide a stimulus shelter? At the very least, caregivers should identify which rooms or activity areas are the quietest and the farthest away from normal traffic flow. This area could be used for special quiet activities when having the child's attention is important; for example, reading to children. Similarly, if a child is actively exploring a toy, the stimulus shelter might be an appropriate place for this activity. The child will have a chance to fully explore the toy away from potential interference from other children.

7. Remember that although the physical environment is important, the presence of caregivers is equally important. The ideal environment for a child would be one in which coordination exists between the caregiver and the physical environment. Thus, if a caregiver sees a child beginning to explore a toy actively in a noisy, crowded room, the caregiver may want to guide the child to a stimulus shelter to be away from the noise and the possible interference from other children. Insofar as possible, caregivers should accurately observe their children and the environment. For example, if the caregiver notes that a child is playing less and less with an object, this might be the time to replace it with a new one. Similarly, if a caregiver cannot hear what a child is saying, that might be a sign

that the environment is too noisy, a situation that may interfere with the caregiver's responsivity to the child. When caregivers coordinate their activities with the characteristics of the physical environment, their children's intellectual development will be optimal.

References

The sources listed below are professional and technical references on the physical environment and early development.

Cohen, S.; G. Evans; D. Stokols; and D. Krantz. (1986). *Behavior, health, and environmental stress.* New York: Plenum Publishing Corporation.

Diamond, M. (1988). *Enriching heredity: The impact of the environment on the anatomy of the brain.* New York: Free Press.

McSwain, R. (1981). Care and conflict in infant development. *Infant Behavior and Development,* 4, 225–46.

Wachs, Theodore D. (1986). Models of physical environment action. In *Play interactions: The contribution of play materials and parental involvement to child development.* Edited by A. Gottfried and C. Brown. Lexington, Mass.: D. C. Heath and Company; distributed by Macmillan Publishing Co., Inc.

Wachs, Theodore D. (1990). Must the physical environment be mediated by the social environment in order to influence development? A further test. *Journal of Applied Developmental Psychology,* 11, 163–78.

Wachs, Theodore D., and A. Chan. (1986). Specificity of environmental action as seen in environmental correlates of infant's communication performance. *Child Development,* Vol. 57, No. 6 (December), 1464–74.

Wachs, Theodore D., and G. Gruen. (1982). *Early experience and human development.* New York: Plenum Publishing Corporation.

Wohlwill, Joachim, and H. Heft. (1987). The physical environment and the development of the child. In *Handbook of environmental psychology.* Vol. 1. Edited by D. Stokols and I. Altman. New York: John Wiley and Sons, Inc.

The sources listed below are nontechnical references.

McGregor, S. (1980). *Toys you can make for children under two.* Kingston, Jamaica, West Indies.

McGregor, S. (1980). *Toys you can make for children under four.* Kingston, Jamaica, West Indies. (Both publications are available from Tropical Metabolism Research Unit, University of the West Indies, Mona, Kingston 7. Jamaica, West Indies.)

Note: In support of this article, this addendum provides additional materials that have been published since the original publication of the guide.

Greenman, James, and Anne Stonehouse. (1997). *Prime times: a handbook for excellence in infant and toddler programs.* St. Paul: Red Leaf Press.

Stephenson, Alison. (2002). "What George taught me about toddlers and water." *Young Children,* 57 (May), 10–14.

Weinberg, Nanci. (2000). "Overcoming obstacles to create retreats in family child care." *Young Children,* 55 (September), 78–81.

Caregivers' Practices That Support Positive Learning Environments

The visions listed here are excerpts from Vision VII in *Visions for Infant/Toddler Care: Guidelines for Professional Caregiving* (see also p. 34 in this guide, "Learning Environment: Vision Statement").

Vision: Children of all ages learn through their own experiences, trial and error, repetition, and imitation. Adults can guide and encourage children's learning by ensuring that the environment is emotionally appropriate; invites play, active exploration, and movement by children; and supports a broad array of experiences. A reliable framework of routines, together with a stimulating choice of activities and materials, facilitates children's learning. Thoughtful caregivers recognize that the learning environment includes both people and relationships between people and that attention to the way in which environments are set up and used is an important contribution to the quality of a learning experience.

Practices: The infant/toddler caregiver working in a center or family day care home:

- Uses materials, books, and equipment that are stimulating to each child and suitable to individual learning styles, including those of handicapped children
- Uses materials that demonstrate support for each child's sex, family, race, language, and culture
- Provides easily accessible learning materials (for example, puzzles, crayons, or books) that children can explore by themselves as well as puts some materials away for special times or for use at later stages of development
- Organizes space into identifiable areas that encourage appropriate and independent use of materials
- Builds a positive social and emotional environment supportive of children's learning

- Balances activities that are active and quiet, free and structured, individual and group focused, and indoors and outdoors
- Provides many opportunities for children to develop their senses and ability to concentrate
- Observes children as individuals and in groups frequently and modifies the environment to meet their changing abilities, needs, and interests
- Varies routines spontaneously to take advantage of unusual opportunities; for example, goes outside in the snow, invites a visiting grandmother to share stories or songs with children, lets the children watch workers and machinery on the street, or plays with one child for an extra period of time when additional adults are available to care for the group
- Supports relationships between adults and children, as well as between children in care, as an important aspect of the learning environment
- Schedules the day to provide time for individual attention to each child
- Encourages children to become involved in activities that extend their attention spans
- Provides simple and consistent routines for mealtimes, naps, preparation to go outdoors, changing activities, clean up, and so forth, supporting children's learning through the routines
- Makes and helps parents to make toys and equipment from easily available materials for use in the home and center

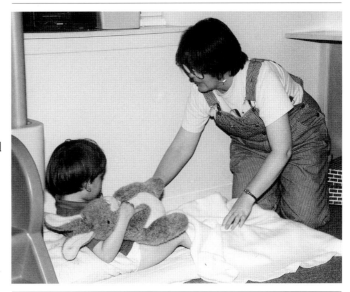

Vision: *Young infants* (birth to nine months) begin to learn from their immediate surroundings and daily experiences. The sense of well-being and emotional security conveyed by a loving and skilled caregiver creates a readiness for other experiences. Before infants can creep and crawl, caregivers should provide a variety of sensory experiences and encourage movement and playfulness.

Practices: The caregiver working with *young infants* also:

- Changes an infant's position and location often during the day and responds to the child's developing skills, such as sitting up, rolling over, reaching for objects, and making noises

- Provides a learning environment for nonmobile infants that encourages mouthing, reaching, batting, grasping, babbling, and social interaction
- Understands and respects the individual needs of infants for eating and sleeping
- Carries the child about frequently in arms, on a hip, or in a sling
- Takes the infant outdoors to experience various temperatures and variations in light, breezes, and so forth
- Provides the infant with the sights and sounds of other living things—humans, animals, and plants—including the caregiver's own face
- Recognizes the importance of a consistent relationship between a caregiver and an infant and makes interaction between the caregiver and child the base of the infant's learning environment

Vision: *Mobile infants* (six to eighteen months) are active, independent, and curious. They are increasingly persistent and purposeful in doing things. They need many opportunities to practice new skills and explore the environment within safe boundaries. Adults can share children's delight in themselves, their skills, and discoveries and gradually add variety to the learning environment.

Practices: The caregiver working with *mobile infants* also:

- Arranges a room so that mobile infants have an area in which to move freely and be protected from older children
- "Baby-proofs" the environment to provide many opportunities for child-initiated learning and to minimize setting limits
- Understands that intense feelings and rapid changes in mood and energy influence the child's response to the environment and adjusts routines, activities, and materials supportively

Vision: *Toddlers* (sixteen to thirty-six months) are developing new language skills, physical control, and awareness of themselves and others each day. They enjoy participation in planned and group activities, but they are not ready to sit still or work in a group for very long. Adults can support the toddlers' learning in all areas by maintaining an environment that is dependable but flexible enough to provide opportunities for them to extend their skills, understanding, and judgment in individual ways.

Practices: The caregiver working with *toddlers* also:

- Expands the learning environment to include the community when possible; for example, trips to the local shops, walks around the block, or attendance at community events
- Introduces a variety of materials and opportunities for learning based on an understanding of toddlers' developmental levels, abilities, and interests; for example, provides water play in an area that can get wet, covers children's clothes with plastic smocks or removes clothing in warm weather, and limits such play to a few children so that each has plenty of room and free use of utensils

- Provides a step stool when necessary so that children can use the toilet and wash their hands independently as soon as possible

Practices: The caregiver working in a family child care home also:

- Provides opportunities for older and younger children to play together
- Teaches children to respect the space and belongings of family members and other children in care
- Allows children to explore and play with safe household materials and everyday objects, such as pots and pans, magazines, and empty cartons
- Helps children learn from watching adult activities, asking questions, and helping adults when they can
- Limits the time when television is on, chooses programs appropriate for young children, and talks with children about what they see and hear

Section Three:
Developmental Milestones

Developmental Milestones of Children from Birth to Age Three

The following developmental milestones are approximations at best. Caregivers need to remember that great individual differences exist among children and that early cognitive development and learning are not necessarily associated with later development. The source for the milestones cited in this section is *Developmentally Appropriate Practice in Early Childhood Programs Serving Children from Birth Through Age 8.* Edited by Sue Bredekamp. Washington, D.C.: National Association for the Education of Young Children, 1987, pp. 30–31. Reprinted by permission from the National Center for Clinical Infant Programs (NCCIP), Arlington, Virginia.

Interest in Others

The Early Months (Birth Through Eight Months of Age)

- Newborns prefer the human face and human sound. Within the first two weeks, they recognize and prefer the sight, smell, and sound of the principal caregiver.
- Social smile and mutual gazing is evidence of early social interaction. The infant can initiate and terminate these interactions.
- Anticipates being lifted or fed and moves the body to participate.
- Sees adults as objects of interest and novelty. Seeks out adults for play. Stretches arms to be taken.

Crawlers and Walkers (Eight to Eighteen Months of Age)

- Exhibits anxious behavior around unfamiliar adults.
- Enjoys exploring objects with another as the basis for establishing relationships.

- Gets others to do things for child's pleasure (wind up toys, read books, get dolls).
- Shows considerable interest in peers.
- Demonstrates intense attention to adult language.

Toddlers and Two-Year-Olds (Eighteen Months to Three Years of Age)

- Shows increased awareness of being seen and evaluated by others.
- Sees others as a barrier to immediate gratification.
- Begins to realize others have rights and privileges.
- Gains greater enjoyment from peer play and joint exploration.
- Begins to see benefits of cooperation.
- Identifies self with children of the same age or sex.
- Is more aware of the feelings of others.
- Exhibits more impulse control and self-regulation in relation to others.
- Enjoys small group activities.

Self-awareness

The Early Months (Birth Through Eight Months of Age)

- Sucks fingers or hand fortuitously.
- Observes own hands.
- Places hand up as an object comes close to the face as if to protect self.
- Looks to the place on body where being touched.
- Reaches for and grasps toys.
- Clasps hands together and fingers them.
- Tries to cause things to happen.
- Begins to distinguish friends from strangers. Shows preference for being held by familiar people.

Crawlers and Walkers (Eight to Eighteen Months of Age)

- Knows own name.
- Smiles or plays with self in mirror.
- Uses large and small muscles to explore confidently when a sense of security is offered by presence of caregiver. Frequently checks for caregiver's presence.
- Has heightened awareness of opportunities to make things happen, yet limited awareness of responsibility for own actions.
- Indicates strong sense of self through assertiveness. Directs actions of others (e.g., "Sit there!").
- Identifies one or more body parts.
- Begins to use *me, you, I.*

Toddlers and Two-Year-Olds (Eighteen Months to Three Years of Age)

- Shows a strong sense of self as an individual, as evidenced by "NO" to adult requests.
- Experiences self as a powerful, potent, creative doer. Explores everything.
- Becomes capable of self-evaluation and has beginning notions of self (good, bad, attractive, ugly).
- Makes attempts at self-regulation.
- Uses names of self and others.
- Identifies six or more body parts.

Physical, Spatial, and Temporal Awareness

The Early Months (Birth Through Eight Months of Age)

- Comforts self by sucking thumb or finding pacifier.
- Follows a slowly moving object with eyes.
- Reaches and grasps toys.
- Looks for dropped toy.
- Identifies objects from various viewpoints. Finds a toy hidden under a blanket when placed there while watching.

Crawlers and Walkers (Eight to Eighteen Months of Age)

- Tries to build with blocks.
- If toy is hidden under one of three cloths while child watches, looks under the right cloth for the toy.
- Persists in a search for a desired toy even when toy is hidden under distracting objects such as pillows.
- When chasing a ball that rolled under sofa and out the other side, will make a detour around sofa to get ball.
- Pushes foot into shoe, arm into sleeve.

Toddlers and Two-Year-Olds (Eighteen Months to Three Years of Age)

- Identifies a familiar object by touch when placed in a bag with two other objects.
- Uses "tomorrow," "yesterday."

- Figures out which child is missing by looking at children who are present.
- Asserts independence: "Me do it."
- Puts on simple garments, such as cap or slippers.

Purposeful Action and Use of Tools

The Early Months (Birth Through Eight Months of Age)

- Observes own hands.
- Grasps rattle when the hand and rattle are both in view.
- Hits or kicks an object to make a pleasing sight or sound continue.
- Tries to resume a knee ride by bouncing to get adult started again.

Crawlers and Walkers (Eight to Eighteen Months of Age)

- When a toy winds down, continues the activity manually.
- Uses a stick as a tool to obtain a toy.
- When a music box winds down, searches for the key to wind it up again.

- Brings a stool to use for reaching for something.
- Pushes away someone or something not wanted.
- Feeds self finger food (bits of fruit, crackers).
- Creeps or walks to get something or avoid unpleasantness.
- Pushes foot into shoe, arm into sleeve.
- Partially feeds self with fingers or spoon.
- Handles cup well with minimal spilling.
- Handles spoon well for self-feeding.

Toddlers and Two-Year-Olds (Eighteen Months to Three Years of Age)

- When playing with a ring-stacking toy, ignores any forms that have no hole. Stacks only rings or other objects with holes.
- Classifies, labels, and sorts objects by group (hard versus soft, large versus small).
- Helps dress and undress self.

Section Four:
Appropriate and Inappropriate Practices

Introduction

This section describes appropriate and inappropriate practices related to the intellectual growth of young children. The practices are written for caregivers and are divided into two parts, one for infants and one for toddlers. In this section *infants* refers to children who are not yet walking; *toddlers* refers to children from the time they begin walking until they are about three years of age.

The majority of practices listed in this section are excerpted from *Developmentally Appropriate Practice in Early Childhood Programs Serving Children from Birth Through Age 8.* (pp. 35–37, 40–45) by Sue Bredekamp (Ed.), 1987, Washington, D.C.: National Association for the Education of Young Children. Copyright © 1987. Used by permission.

Appropriate and Inappropriate Practices Related to Infants

In this section *infants* refers to children who are not yet walking.

Appropriate practice	Inappropriate practice
• Caregivers respond quickly to infants' cries or calls of distress, recognizing that crying and body movements are infants' only way to communicate. Responses are soothing and tender.	• Crying is ignored or responded to irregularly at the convenience of the adult. Crying is treated as a nuisance. Adults' responses neglect the infants' needs.
• Playful interactions with babies are done in ways that are sensitive to the child's level of tolerance for physical movement, louder sounds, or other changes.	• Adults frighten, tease, or upset children with their unpredictable behaviors.
• Children's play interests are respected. Adults observe the child's activity and comment, offer additional ideas for play, and encourage the child's engagement in the activity.	• Infants are interrupted, toys are whisked from their grasp, adults impose their own ideas or even play with toys themselves regardless of the child's interest.

Appropriate practice	*Inappropriate practice*
• The caregiver frequently talks with, sings to, and reads to infants. Language is a vital, lively form of communication with individuals.	• Infants are expected to entertain themselves or watch television. Language is used infrequently and vocabularies limited.
• Infants are praised for their accomplishments and helped to feel increasingly competent.	• Infants are criticized for what they cannot do or for their clumsy struggle to master a skill. They are made to feel inadequate and that they have no effect on others.
• Adults frequently engage in games such as Peek-a-Boo and Five Little Piggies with infants who are interested and responsive to the play.	• Games are imposed on children regardless of their interest. Play is seen as a time filler rather than a learning experience.
• Diaper changing, feeding, and other routines are viewed as vital learning experiences for babies.	• Routines are dealt with superficially and indifferently.
• The environment contains both soft (pillows, padded walls) and hard (rocking chairs, mirrors) elements.	• The environment is either sterile or cluttered, but lacks variety.
• The area that is the focus of play changes periodically during the day from the floor, to strollers, to being carried, to rocking or swinging, and other variations to give infants different perspectives on people and places. Children are cared for both indoors and outdoors.	• Babies are confined to cribs, playpens, or the floor for long periods indoors. Time outdoors is viewed as too much bother, or is not done because of excuses about the weather.

Appropriate practice	*Inappropriate practice*
• Mirrors are placed where infants can observe themselves—on the wall next to the floor, next to the diapering area.	• Children never have a chance to see themselves.
• The room is cheerful and decorated at children's eye level with pictures of people's faces, friendly animals, and other familiar objects. Pictures of children and their families are displayed.	• Areas are dingy and dark. Decorations are at adult eye level and are uninteresting. No family photos are displayed.
• A variety of music is provided for enjoyment in listening/body movement/ singing.	• Music is used to distract or lull infants to sleep. Children hear only children's songs.
• Space is arranged so children can enjoy moments of quiet play by themselves, so they have space to roll over, and so they can crawl toward interesting objects.	• Space is cramped and unsafe for children who are learning how to move their bodies.
• Toys are safe, washable, and too large for infants to swallow. They range from very simple to more complex.	• Toys are sharp, tiny, with chipping paint, or otherwise unsafe and not washable. Toys are too simple or too complex for the infants served.
• Toys provided are responsive to the child's actions: bells, busy boards, balls, vinyl-covered pillows to climb on, large beads that snap together, nesting bowls, small blocks, shape sorters, music boxes, squeeze toys that squeak.	• Toys are battery-powered or wind up so the baby just watches. Toys lack a variety of texture, size, and shape.
• Mobiles are designed to be seen from the child's viewpoint. They are removed when children can reach for and grasp them.	• Mobiles are out of infants' vision. They are positioned where children can reach them.
• Toys are scaled to a size that enables infants to grasp, chew, and manipulate them (clutch balls, rattles, spoons, teethers, rubber dolls).	• Toys are too large to handle, or unsafe for children to chew on.

Appropriate practice	*Inappropriate practice*
• Toys are available on open shelves so children can make their own selections.	• Toys are dumped in a box or kept out of children's reach forcing them to depend on adults' selection.
• Books are heavy cardboard with rounded edges. They have bright pictures of familiar objects.	• Books are not available, or are made of paper that tears easily. Books do not contain objects familiar or interesting to children. Faded colors or intricate drawings are used.

Appropriate and Inappropriate Practices Related to Toddlers

In this section *toddlers* refers to children from the time they begin walking until they are about three years of age.

Appropriate practice	*Inappropriate practice*
• Adults engage in many one-to-one, face-to-face conversations with toddlers. Adults let toddlers initiate language, and wait for a response, even from children whose language is limited. Adults label or name objects, describe events, and reflect feelings to help children learn new words. Adults simplify their language for toddlers who are just beginning to talk (instead of "It's time to wash our hands and have snack," the adult says, "Let's wash hands. Snacktime!") Then as children acquire their own words, adults expand on the toddler's language (for example *Toddler*—"Mary sock." *Adult*—"Oh, that's Mary's missing sock, and you found it.").	• Adults talk *at* toddlers and do not wait for a response. Adult voices dominate or adults do not speak to children because they think they are too young to respond. Adults either talk "baby talk" or use language that is too complex for toddlers to understand.

Appropriate practice	Inappropriate practice
• Adults are supportive of toddlers as they acquire skills. Adults watch to see what the child is trying to do and provide the necessary support to help the child accomplish the task, allowing children to do what they are capable of doing and assisting with tasks that are frustrating.	• Adults are impatient and intrusive. They expect too much or too little of toddlers. Because it is faster, adults do tasks for toddlers that children can do themselves. Or adults allow children to become frustrated by tasks they cannot do.
• Adults respond quickly to toddlers' cries or calls for help, recognizing that toddlers have limited language with which to communicate their needs.	• Crying is ignored or responded to irregularly or at the adults' convenience.
• Adults respect toddlers' desire to carry favored objects around with them, to move objects like household items from one place to another, and to roam around or sit and parallel play with toys and objects.	• Adults restrict objects to certain locations and do not tolerate hoarding, collecting, or carrying.
• Children are praised for their accomplishments and helped to feel increasingly competent and in control of themselves.	• Toddlers are criticized for what they cannot do or for their clumsy struggle to master a skill. Or adults foster dependency; children are overprotected and made to feel inadequate.
• Adults recognize that routine tasks of living like eating, toileting, and dressing are important opportunities to help children learn about their world and to regulate their own behavior.	• Routine times are chaotic because all children are expected to do the same thing at the same time.
• Adults play with toddlers reciprocally, modeling for toddlers how to play imaginatively with baby dolls and accessories. For example, adults and children play "tea party," where the adult pretends to drink from a cup and exclaims how good it tastes and then the toddler often models the adult.	• Adults do not play with toddlers because they feel silly or bored.

Appropriate practice	Inappropriate practice
• Adults support toddlers' play so that toddlers stay interested in an object or activity for longer periods of time and their play becomes more complex, moving from simple awareness and exploration of objects to more complicated play like pretending.	• Adults do not think that supporting children's play is important. They do not understand the value of play for learning or they feel silly playing with young children.
• Toddlers' solitary and parallel play is respected. Adults provide several of the same popular toys for children to play with alone or near another child. Adults realize that having three or four of the same sought-after toys is more helpful than having one each of many different toys.	• Adults do not understand the value of solitary and parallel play and try to force children to play together. Adults arbitrarily expect children to share. Popular toys are not provided in duplicate and fought over constantly while other toys are seldom used.
• Adults prepare the environment to allow for predictability and repetition, as well as events that can be expected and anticipated.	• Adults lose patience with doing many of the same things repeatedly and get bored by toddlers' needs to repeat tasks until they master them or feel secure in a predictable environment.
• Adults frequently read to toddlers, individually on laps or in groups of two or three. Adults sing with toddlers, do fingerplays, act out simple stories like "The Three Bears" with children participating actively, or tell stories using a flannelboard or magnetic board, and allow children to manipulate and place figures on the boards.	• Adults impose "group time" on toddlers, forcing a large group to listen or watch an activity without opportunity for children to participate.
• Toddlers are given appropriate art media such as large crayons, watercolor markers, and large paper. Adults expect toddlers to explore and manipulate art materials and do *not* expect them to produce a finished art product. Adults *never* use food for art because toddlers are developing self-regulatory skills and must learn to distinguish between food and other objects that are not to be eaten.	• Toddlers are "helped" by teachers to produce a product, follow the adult-made model, or color a coloring book or ditto sheet. Tactilely sensitive toddlers are required to fingerpaint or are given edible fingerpaint or playdough because they will probably put it in their mouths.

Appropriate practice	*Inappropriate practice*
• Diaper changing, toilet learning, eating, dressing, and other routines are viewed as vital learning experiences.	• Routines are dealt with superficially and indifferently.
• Children have daily opportunities for exploratory activity outdoors, such as water and sand play and easel painting. Water play is available daily, requiring that adults dry clothes or provide clothing changes. Children have opportunities for supervised play in sand. Adults recognize that sand is a soft and absorbing medium ideally suited for toddler exploration. Well-supervised sand play is used to teach children to self-regulate what they can and cannot eat.	• Adults do not offer water and sand play because they are messy and require supervision, using as an excuse that children will get wet or will eat sand. Children's natural enjoyment of water play is frustrated so they play in toilets or at sinks whenever they can.
• Routines are planned as learning experiences to help children become skilled and independent. Meals and snacks include finger food or utensils that are easier for toddlers to use such as bowls, spoons, and graduated versions of drinking objects from bottles to cups. Dressing and undressing are seen as learning activities and children's attempts to dress themselves and put on shoes are supported and positively encouraged.	• Adults foster children's dependence by doing routine tasks for them that they could do for themselves. Children feel incompetent because the eating utensils are too difficult for them or clothes require adult assistance with tiny buttons or laces.
• The environment contains both soft (pillows, padded walls, carpeting) and hard (rocking chairs, mirrors) elements.	• The environment is dominated by hard surfaces because they are easier to keep clean.
• The environment contains private spaces with room for no more than two children.	• The environment provides no private spaces.

Appropriate practice	*Inappropriate practice*
• Children have many opportunities for active, large muscle play both indoors and outdoors. The environment includes ramps and steps that are the correct size for children to practice newly acquired skills. Toddlers' outdoor play space is separate from that of older children. Outdoor play equipment for toddlers includes small climbing equipment that they can go around, in, and out of, and solitary play equipment requiring supervision such as swings and low slides.	• Toddlers' indoor space is cramped and unsafe for children who are just learning how to move their bodies and need to run more than walk. Toddlers share outdoor space and unsafe equipment designed for older children.

• The room is cheerful and decorated at the children's eye level with pictures of faces of people, friendly animals, and other familiar objects. Pictures of children and their families are encouraged.	• Areas are dingy and dark. Decorations are at adult eye levels, or are too syrupy and cute. No evidence exists of personal involvement for families.
• Sturdy picture books are provided. Pictures depict a variety of ages and ethnic groups in a positive way.	• Books are not available because they get torn or soiled. Pictures are cartoons or other stereotypes.
• Toys are available on open shelves so that children can make their own selections. Toys can be carried and moved about in the environment as children choose.	• Toys are dumped in a box or kept away from children's reach so they are at the mercy of the adult's selection. Adults attempt to restrict the use of toys to certain areas, like housekeeping or blocks.

Section Five:
Suggested Resources

Suggested Resources

Books and Articles

Bromwich, Rose. "Learning and Growth Experiences for Infants," in *Setting up for Infant Care: Guidelines for Centers and Family Child Care Homes* (Revised edition). Edited by Annabelle Godwin and Lorraine Schrag. Washington, D.C.: National Association for the Education of Young Children, 1988, pp. 10–16.

This article provides an overview of issues to consider in supporting the learning and growth of infants. It addresses the importance to infants of continuity of care, adult-child interaction, child-child interaction, and play. It offers many practical ideas and guidelines.

Caulfield, Rick. "Physical and Cognitive Development in the First Two Years," *Early Childhood Education Journal,* Vol. 23 (1996), 239–42.

The first in a four-part series on the development of infants and toddlers, these articles focus on physical, cognitive, social, and emotional development as well as caregiving issues, partnership with the family, and the professionalism of in-home and center-based early care.

Dodge, Diane Trister; Amy L. Dombro; and Derry G. Koralek. "Module 5: Cognitive: What Is Cognitive Develop-ment and Why Is It Important?" in *Caring for Infants and Toddlers,* Vol. 1. Washington, D.C.: Teaching Strategies, Inc., 1991.

This article presents ideas to consider when caring for infants and toddlers in groups and offers checklists and practical exercises to help caregivers become aware of ways to facilitate early cognitive development. It relates cognitive development to other developmental domains.

From Neurons to Neighborhoods: The Science of Early Childhood Development. Edited by Jack P. Shonkoff and Deborah A. Phillips. Washington, D.C.: National Academy Press, 2000.

This book synthesizes the literature, elaborates on a number of core concepts of development, and offers recommendations for policy and practice.

Greenspan, Stanley I. *Intelligence and Adaptation.* Madison, Conn.: International Universities Press, Inc., 1980.

This book explores the relationship between emotional and cognitive or intellectual development during infancy within a unified framework. It emphasizes the psychoanalytic model and Jean Piaget's model of early development.

Gonzalez-Mena, Janet, and Dianne W. Eyer. *Infants, Toddlers, and Caregivers.* Mountain View, Calif.: Mayfield Publishing Co., 1989, pp. 107–17.

This book presents in a highly readable form stages of cognitive development during infancy. It discusses security and attachment as prerequisites for cognitive development and considers why teaching academic kinds of experience to infants and toddlers is inappropriate.

Infant/Toddler Caregiving: A Guide to Culturally Sensitive Care. Sacramento: California Department of Education, 1993.

This guide illuminates the role of culture in early learning and development and offers suggestions on how caregivers can go about adapting their care to the cultural experiences of infants. It examines the role of culture in early learning and the ways in which the handling of caregiving routines varies from culture to culture.

Infant/Toddler Caregiving: A Guide to Language Development and Communication. Sacramento: California Department of Education, 1990.

This guide explores how to support the development of language and communication during the young, mobile, and older periods of infancy and discusses the impact of bilingual and cultural experiences on language development. It considers the influences of social interaction, general learning activities, and materials and toys in language development.

Infant/Toddler Caregiving: A Guide to Routines. (Second edition). Sacramento: California Department of Education, 1990.

This guide covers the full range of caregiving routines. Attention is given to the social-emotional climate in which routines are carried out and the types of learning experiences that routines make available to children.

Infant/Toddler Caregiving: A Guide to Setting Up Environments. Sacramento: California Department of Education, 1990.

This guide presents detailed information on issues to consider and practical guidelines to follow in setting up a group care environment for infants and toddlers. It examines many topics related to intellectual development and creativity, including exploration, choice, variety, and overstimulation of infants.

Infant/Toddler Caregiving: A Guide to Social-Emotional Growth and Socialization. Sacramento: California Department of Education, 1990.

This guide presents an overview of infant temperament, emotional milestones, responsive caregiving, emotional nurturance, guidance, and socialization. It explores the meaning of children's fantasy and make-believe play and the relationship between cognitive development and social-emotional well-being.

Meltzoff, Andrew M. "Infant Imitation and Memory: Nine-Month-Olds in Immediate and Deferred Tests," *Child Development,* Vol. 59 (1988), 217–25.

This article describes a study of the ability of nine-month-old infants to imitate simple actions with novel objects. The study provides a largely untapped method for investigating the nature and development of recall memory in the preverbal child.

Murphy, Lois Barclay. "Creativity in the Youngest," *Zero to Three Journal,* Vol. 17 (December 1996/January 1997), 35–36.

The article discusses very young children's creativity—both their early spontaneous expressions of feeling through movement and art materials and their use of creativity as a way of coping with frustration and pain.

Sawyers, Janet K., and Cosby S. Rogers. "Helping Babies Play," *Young Children,* Vol. 13 (1988), 13–21.

This book excerpt briefly notes the typical developmental features of babies ages birth to four months, four to eight months, eight to twelve months, and twelve to eighteen months. The authors make suggestions for interactions supporting play during each stage.

Stokes Szanton, Eleanor. "For America's Infants and Toddlers, Are Important Values Threatened by our Zeal to 'Teach'?" *Young Children,* Vol. 56 (January 2001), 15–21.

This article explores the idea that national characteristics may be unintentionally threatened if child care programs ignore choice, exploration, and self-expression.

Thoman, Evelyn B., and Sue Browder. *Born Dancing: How Intuitive Parents Understand Their Baby's Unspoken Language and Natural Rhythms.* New York: HarperCollins Publishers, 1988.

Written primarily for parents, this book contains information about a perspective on infancy that caregivers find useful. It presents a philosophy of caregiving based on respect and responsive interaction with infants and advises against formal teaching.

Wein, Carol Anne, and Susan Kirby-Smith. "Untiming the Curriculum: A Case Study of Removing Clocks from the Program," *Young Children,* Vol. 53 (September 1998), 8–13.

This article describes two teachers in a toddler program who stop regimenting the children's schedule according to the clock. Instead of being dictated by a production schedule, children engage in activities as long as their interest lasts. The result leads to a creative curriculum, more complex play, and freedom to learn.

Whitehead, Linda C., and Stanley Greenspan. "Creating a Family-like Atmosphere in Child Care Settings: All the More Difficult in Large Child Care Centers," *Young Children,* Vol. 54 (March 1999), 4–10.

This article describes some ways to create a family-like atmosphere in early childhood centers. The authors discuss the physical space, curriculum, schedule, and family interactions.

Zeavin, Carol. "Toddlers at Play: Environments at Work," *Young Children,* Vol. 52 (March 1997), 72–77.

This article presents eight vignettes that illustrate how time, space, materials, and relationships contribute to a quality program and to toddlers' well-being.

Audiovisual Materials

The Ages of Infancy: Caring for Young, Mobile, and Older Infants. Sacramento: California Department of Education, 1990. Videocassette, color, 26 minutes; printed text.

This video divides infancy into three age-related stages of development: young infants (birth to eight months of age), mobile infants (six to eighteen months of age), and older infants (sixteen to thirty-six months of age). It describes ways caregivers can help children with the issues of security, exploration, and identity in each of the three stages of development. Videocassette available in English, Spanish, and Chinese (Cantonese).

Discoveries of Infancy: Cognitive Development and Learning. Sacramento: California Department of Education, 1992. Videocassette, color, 32 minutes; printed text.

This video illustrates six discoveries of infancy: things don't disappear, cause and effect, the use of tools, imitation, space, and the way things are best used. It offers suggestions about how caregivers can support cognitive development. Videocassette available in English, Spanish, and Chinese (Cantonese).

Early Messages: Facilitating Language Development and Communication. Sacramento: California Department of Education, 1998. Videocassette, color, 28 minutes; printed text.

This video opens by describing infants' biologically built-in potential to learn language and underscores that early communication is rooted in the child's family and culture.

Flexible, Fearful, or Fiesty: The Different Temperaments of Infants and Toddlers. Sacramento: California Department of Education, 1990. Videocassette, color, 29 minutes; printed text.

This video explores various temperamental styles of infants and toddlers. It groups nine identified traits into three temperamental styles: flexible, fearful, or feisty and describes techniques for dealing with infants and toddlers of different temperaments. Videocassette available in English, Spanish, and Chinese (Cantonese).

Getting in Tune: Creating Nurturing Relationships with Infants and Toddlers. Sacramento: California Department of Education, 1990. Videocassette, color, 24 minutes; printed text.

This video explores steps caregivers can take to learn to become more responsive to infants and toddlers and demonstrates the responsive process of watching, asking, and adapting to the infant. Videocassette available in English, Spanish, and Chinese (Cantonese).

It's Not Just Routine: Feeding, Diapering, and Napping Infants and Toddlers (Second edition). Sacramento: California Department of Education, 2000. Videocassette, color, 28 minutes; printed text.

This video presents issues to consider in setting up and carrying out the caregiving routines of feeding, diapering, napping and ways to lower the risk of SIDS (sudden infant death syndrome), and the proper use of protective gloves. It provides examples of caregivers being responsive to the child and creating opportunities for learning. Videocassette available in English, Spanish, and Chinese (Cantonese).

A Journey Through the First Year of Life. New York: American Baby Cable. Videocassette, 50 minutes.

This video charts the physical, cognitive, language, and social-emotional development of babies. It reminds caregivers to take time to observe infants, to learn about their emerging skills, and to be loving and attentive toward them.

The Next Step: Including the Infant in the Curriculum. Sacramento: California Department of Education, 2002. Videocassctte, color 22 minutes; printed text.

This video offers the research, theory, and tried-and-true caregiver practices that support optimal learning in children under three years of age. Videocassette available in English and Spanish.

Respectfully Yours: Magda Gerber's Approach to Professional Infant/ Toddler Care. Sacramento: California Department of Education, 1988. Videocassette, color, 58 minutes; printed text.

This video presents an interview of infant care expert Magda Gerber by J. Ronald Lally. It gives an overview of Magda Gerber's philosophy of care that emphasizes respecting and giving full attention to infants and toddlers. Videocassette available in English, Spanish, and Chinese (Cantonese).

Space to Grow: Creating a Child Care Environment for Infants and Toddlers (Second edition). Sacramento: California Department of Education, 2004. Videocassette, color, 38 minutes; printed text.

The second edition of this video illustrates eight major concepts to consider in setting up environments for infants and toddlers and shows how the environment can be arranged to support relationships as well as early learning and development. Videocassette available in English, Spanish, and Chinese (Cantonese).

Thought. The Toddler Series. 1977. Filmstrip/Audiocassette, color, 10 minutes.

This filmstrip shows the growing abilities of toddlers to reason, remember, imagine, anticipate, and analyze, particularly as they become able to use signs and symbols in their thinking. It illustrates how to promote creativity in children and discusses the importance of fantasy and make-believe for toddlers.

New Resources on Brain Development

In the last ten years, much information on brain development has emerged that supports the information in this guide. A list of key references is provided below.

Anzalone, Marie E., and Gordon Williamson. *Sensory Integration and Self-Regulation in Infants and Toddlers.* Washington, D.C.: Zero to Three, 2001.

Bloom, L., and others. "Early Conversations and Word Learning: Contributions from Child and Adult," *Child Development,* Vol. 67 (1996), 3154–175.

Diamond, Marian, and Janet Hopson. *Magic Trees of the Mind.* New York: Dutton, 1998.

Greenspan, Stanley I. *The Growth of the Mind.* New York: Addison-Wesley Publishing, 1997.

Gunnar, Megan. "Quality of Care and the Buffering of Stress Physiology: Its Potential Role in Protecting the Developing Human Brain." Address given at the Zero to Three Eleventh National Training Institute, Washington, D.C., December 7, 1996.

Hart, Betty, and Todd R. Risley. *Meaningful Differences in Everyday Experience of Young American Children.* Baltimore: Paul H. Brookes Publishing Co., 1995.

Karr-Morse, Robin, and Meredith S. Wiley. *Ghosts from the Nursery: Tracing the Roots of Violence.* New York: Atlantic Monthly Press, 1997.

Hawley, Theresa. "Ready to Succeed: The Lasting Effects of Early Relationships." Ounce of Prevention Fund and Zero to Three Paper, 1998.

Hawley, Theresa. "Starting Smart: How Early Experiences Affect Brain Development." Chicago: An Ounce of Prevention Fund and Zero to Three Paper, 1996.

Kuhl, P. K., and others. "Cross-Language Analysis of Phonetic Units in Language Addressed to Infants," *Science,* Vol. 277 (August 1997), 684–88.

Lally, J. Ronald. "Research, Infant Learning, and Child Care Curriculum," *Child Care Information Exchange,* (May 1998), 46–48.

Lally, J. Ronald. "Brain Development in Infancy: A Critical Period," *Bridges,* Vol. 3 (1997), 4–6.

Lally, J. Ronald. "Effects of Maternal Depression on Emotional Development of Infants and Toddlers," *Bridges,* Vol. 3 (1997), 7.

Nash, J. Madeleine. "Fertile Minds," *Time,* Vol. 149 (February 1997), 48–56.

Shore, R. *Rethinking the Brain: New Insights into Early Development.* New York: Families and Work Institute, 1997.

Siegel, Daniel J. *The Developing Mind.* New York: The Guilford Press, 1999.

Zigler, Edward F. *The First Three Years and Beyond: Brain Development and Social Policy.* New Haven, Conn.: Yale University Press, 2003.

Audiovisual Materials

Food for Thought/Alimento Intelectual. Shoreview, Minn.: Health Partners, Reading RX. Videocassette, color, 14 minutes.

Ten Things Every Child Needs. Chicago, Ill.: Robert R. McCormick Tribune Foundation. Videocassette, color, 60 minutes.

"I Am Your Child: The First Years Last Forever." CD-ROM (1997). International Business Machines, Inc., and Families and Work Institute. (212-465-2044).

Web Sites

http://www.iamyourchild.org/

http://www.dana.org/brainweek

http://www.kidscampaigns.org

http://www.childtrauma.org/

http://www.zerotothree.org/brainwonders/

MODULE I: Social–Emotional Growth and Socialization

Videos and Video Magazines:
- First Moves: Welcoming a Child to a New Caregiving Setting
- Flexible, Fearful, or Feisty: The Different Temperaments of Infants and Toddlers
- Getting in Tune: Creating Nurturing Relationships with Infants and Toddlers

Printed Materials:
- Infant/Toddler Caregiving: A Guide to Social–Emotional Growth and Socialization
- Module I Trainer's Manual

MODULE II: Group Care

Videos and Video Magazines:
- It's Not Just Routine: Feeding, Diapering, and Napping Infants and Toddlers (Second edition)
- Respectfully Yours: Magda Gerber's Approach to Professional Infant/Toddler Care
- Space to Grow: Creating a Child Care Environment for Infants and Toddlers (Second edition)
- Together in Care: Meeting the Intimacy Needs of Infants and Toddlers in Groups

Printed Materials:
- Infant/Toddler Caregiving: A Guide to Routines (Second edition)
- Infant/Toddler Caregiving: A Guide to Setting Up Environments
- Module II Trainer's Manual

MODULE III: Learning and Development

Videos and Video Magazines:
- The Ages of Infancy: Caring for Young, Mobile, and Older Infants
- Discoveries of Infancy: Cognitive Development and Learning
- Early Messages: Facilitating Language Development and Communication

Printed Materials:
- Infant/Toddler Caregiving: A Guide to Cognitive Development and Learning
- Infant/Toddler Caregiving: A Guide to Language Development and Communication
- Module III Trainer's Manual

MODULE IV: Culture, Family, and Providers

Videos and Video Magazines:
- Essential Connections: Ten Keys to Culturally Sensitive Child Care
- Protective Urges: Working with the Feelings of Parents and Caregivers

Printed Materials:
- Infant/Toddler Caregiving: A Guide to Creating Partnerships with Parents
- Infant/Toddler Caregiving: A Guide to Culturally Sensitive Care
- Module IV Trainer's Manual

ORDER FORM

Title	Item no.	Quantity	Price	Total
Module I: Social–Emotional Growth and Socialization				
First Moves - English video (1988)	0751		$75.00	
First Moves - Spanish video (1988)	0771		75.00	
First Moves - Chinese (Cantonese) video (1988)	0772		75.00	
First Moves - PAL English video (1988)	1416		75.00	
Flexible, Fearful, or Feisty - English video (1990)	0839		75.00	
Flexible, Fearful, or Feisty - Spanish video (1990)	0872		75.00	
Flexible, Fearful, or Feisty - Chinese (Cantonese) video (1990)	0871		75.00	
Flexible, Fearful, or Feisty - PAL English video (1990)	1417		75.00	
Getting in Tune - English video (1990)	0809		75.00	
Getting in Tune - Spanish video (1990)	0811		75.00	
Getting in Tune - Chinese (Cantonese) video (1990)	0810		75.00	
Getting in Tune - PAL English video (1990)	1418		75.00	
Infant/Toddler Caregiving: A Guide to Social–Emotional Growth and Socialization	0876		18.00	
Module I Trainer's Manual	1084		25.00	
Module I: Social–Emotional Growth and Socialization (The package price includes 3 videos, 3 accompanying video magazines, 1 curriculum guide, and 1 trainer's manual.)			**Special price**	
English videos	9928		**239.00**	
Spanish videos	9929		**239.00**	
Chinese (Cantonese) videos	9930		**239.00**	
PAL English videos	9728		**239.00**	

Title	Item no.	Quantity	Price	Total
Module II: Group Care				
It's Not Just Routine - (Second edition) English video (2000)	1483		75.00	
It's Not Just Routine - (Second edition) Spanish video (2000)	1484		75.00	
It's Not Just Routine - (Second edition) Chinese (Cantonese) video (2000)	1485		75.00	
It's Not Just Routine - (Second edition) PAL English video (2000)	1506		75.00	
Respectfully Yours - English video (1988)	0753		75.00	
Respectfully Yours - Spanish video (1988)	0773		75.00	
Respectfully Yours - Chinese (Cantonese) video (1988)	0774		75.00	
Respectfully Yours - PAL English video (1988)	1422		75.00	
Space to Grow - (Second edition) English video (2004)	1595		75.00	
Space to Grow - (Second edition) Spanish video (2004)	1596		75.00	
Space to Grow - PAL English video (2004)	1423		75.00	
Together in Care - English video (1992)	1044		75.00	
Together in Care - Spanish video (1992)	0888		75.00	
Together in Care - Chinese (Cantonese) video (1992)	1051		75.00	
Together in Care - PAL English video (1992)	1424		75.00	
Infant/Toddler Caregiving: A Guide to Routines (Second edition)	1510		18.00	
Infant/Toddler Caregiving: A Guide to Setting Up Environments	0879		18.00	
Module II Trainer's Manual	1076		25.00	
Module II: Group Care (The package price includes 4 videos, 4 accompanying video magazines, 2 curriculum guides, and 1 trainer's manual.)			**Special price**	
English videos	9931		**319.00**	
Spanish videos	9932		**319.00**	
Chinese (Cantonese) videos (Does not include Space to Grow video)	9933		**249.00**	
PAL English videos	9729		**319.00**	

Note: All videos include a video magazine in English.

Title	Item no.	Quantity	Price	Total
The Ages of Infancy - English video (1990)	0883		$75.00	
The Ages of Infancy - Spanish video (1990)	0884		75.00	
The Ages of Infancy - Chinese (Cantonese) video (1990)	0885		75.00	
The Ages of Infancy - PAL English video (1990)	1413		75.00	
Discoveries of Infancy - English video (1992)	1045		75.00	
Discoveries of Infancy - Spanish video (1992)	0829		75.00	
Discoveries of Infancy - Chinese (Cantonese) video (1992)	0784		75.00	
Discoveries of Infancy - PAL English video (1992)	1414		75.00	
Early Messages - English video (1998)	1425		75.00	
Early Messages - Spanish video (1998)	1446		75.00	
Early Messages - Chinese (Cantonese) video (1998)	1447		75.00	
Early Messages - PAL English video (1998)	1426		75.00	
Infant/Toddler Caregiving: A Guide to Cognitive Development and Learning	1055		18.00	
Infant/Toddler Caregiving: A Guide to Language Development and Communication	0880		18.00	
Module III Trainer's Manual	1108		25.00	
Module III: Learning and Development (The package price includes 3 videos, 3 accompanying video magazines, 2 curriculum guides, and 1 trainer's manual.)			**Special price**	
English videos	9860		**249.00**	
Spanish videos	9861		**249.00**	
Chinese (Cantonese) videos	9862		**249.00**	
PAL English videos	9730		**249.00**	
Essential Connections - English video (1993)	1056		75.00	
Essential Connections - Spanish video (1993)	1058		75.00	
Essential Connections - Chinese (Cantonese) video (1993)	1059		75.00	
Essential Connections - PAL English video (1993)	1415		75.00	
Protective Urges - English video (1996)	1270		75.00	
Protective Urges - Spanish video (1996)	1271		75.00	
Protective Urges - Chinese (Cantonese) video (1996)	1272		75.00	
Protective Urges - PAL English video (1996)	1421		75.00	
Infant/Toddler Caregiving: A Guide to Creating Partnerships with Parents	0878		18.00	
Infant/Toddler Caregiving: A Guide to Culturally Sensitive Care	1057		18.00	
Module IV Trainer's Manual	1109		25.00	
Module IV: Culture, Family, and Providers (The package price includes 2 videos, 2 accompanying video magazines, 2 curriculum guides, and 1 trainer's manual.)			**Special price**	
English videos	9774		**189.00**	
Spanish videos	9775		**189.00**	
Chinese (Cantonese) videos	9776		**189.00**	
PAL English videos	9731		**189.00**	
Talking Points for Essential Connections - English video (1998)	1370		35.00	
Talking Points for Essential Connections - PAL English video (1998)	1427		35.00	
Talking Points for Protective Urges - English video (1998)	1369		25.00	
Talking Points for Protective Urges - PAL English video (1998)	1428		25.00	
Talking Points for Essential Connections - 50 video magazines (English)	9744		23.00	
Talking Points for Protective Urges - 50 video magazines (English)	9743		23.00	
Addendum to Trainer's Manuals I, II, III, IV: Spanish handouts/transparencies	1395		25.00	
The Family Day Care Supplement to Trainer's Manuals	7096		25.00	
In Our Hands - English video (1997)	1432		25.00	
In Our Hands - PAL English video (1997)	1419		25.00	
In Our Hands - 50 video magazines (English) (1997)	9747		23.00	
The Next Step - English video, 22 minutes (2004)	1554		75.00	
The Next Step - Spanish video, 22 minutes (2004)	1593		75.00	
The Next Step - English video, 8.5 minutes (2004)	1594		25.00	
The Next Step - 50 video magazines (English)	9711		23.00	

Module III: Learning and Development

Module IV: Culture, Family, and Providers

Additional Materials Available in The Program

77

Video Magazines

Title	Item no.	Quantity	Price	Total
The Ages of Infancy - 50 video magazines (English)	9954		$23.00	
The Ages of Infancy - 50 video magazines (Spanish)	9732		23.00	
Discoveries of Infancy - 50 video magazines (English)	9874		23.00	
Discoveries of Infancy - 50 video magazines (Spanish)	9733		23.00	
Early Messages - 50 video magazines (English)	9747		23.00	
Early Messages - 50 video magazines (Spanish)	9734		23.00	
Essential Connections - 50 video magazines (English)	9869		23.00	
Essential Connections - 50 video magazines (Spanish)	9735		23.00	
First Moves - 50 video magazines (English)	9960		23.00	
First Moves - 50 video magazines (Spanish)	9736		23.00	
Flexible, Fearful, or Feisty - 50 video magazines (English)	9956		23.00	
Flexible, Fearful, or Feisty - 50 video magazines (Spanish)	9737		23.00	
Getting in Tune - 50 video magazines (English)	9957		23.00	
Getting in Tune - 50 video magazines (Spanish)	9738		23.00	
It's Not Just Routine - 50 video magazines (Second edition) (English)	9724		23.00	
It's Not Just Routine - 50 video magazines (Second edition) (Spanish)	9723		23.00	
Protective Urges - 50 video magazines (English)	9778		23.00	
Protective Urges - 50 video magazines (Spanish)	9739		23.00	
Respectfully Yours - 50 video magazines (English)	9958		23.00	
Respectfully Yours - 50 video magazines (Spanish)	9740		23.00	
Space to Grow - 50 video magazines (Second edition) (English)	9709		23.00	
Space to Grow - 50 video magazines (Second edition) (Spanish)	9710		23.00	
Together in Care - 50 video magazines (English)	9873		23.00	
Together in Care - 50 video magazines (Spanish)	9742		23.00	
Sampler pack of 3 video magazines for each video in Modules I, II, III, & IV (English)	9720		23.00	
Sampler pack of 3 video magazines for each video in Modules I, II, III, and IV (Spanish)	9719		23.00	

Order Form

To order call: 1-800-995-4099   BUSINESS HOURS: 8:00 A.M.–4:30 P.M., PST
MONDAY THROUGH FRIDAY • FAX 916-323-0823

SUBTOTAL $

California residents add sales tax.

Shipping and handling charges (See chart.)

TOTAL $

NAME/ATTENTION

ADDRESS

CITY   STATE   ZIP CODE

(   )

COUNTY   DAYTIME TELEPHONE

PAYMENT METHOD:
☐ CHECK (Payable to California Department of Education)
☐ VISA
☐ MASTERCARD
☐ PURCHASE ORDER

CREDIT CARD NUMBER

EXPIRATION DATE

AUTHORIZED SIGNATURE

No. of Items	Shipping and Handling Charges
1	$3.00
2 - 50	$2.00 per order plus $1.00 per item
51+	Call 1-800-995-4099 for discounted rate

All orders to be delivered within the continental United States are shipped via United Parcel Service (UPS), ground service, ONLY.

UPS requires a street address.

Note: Shipping and handling charges for modules are $5.95 for each module.

Orders to Hawaii and Alaska are shipped via UPS Second Day Air. An additional charge for the shipping cost to those states plus a handling fee will be added to your credit card order.

Visit our Web site: **http://www.cde.ca.gov**

☐ **Please send me a free copy of the current *Educational Resources Catalog*.**

Mail completed order form to:
**California Department of Education
CDE Press Sales Office
1430 N Street, Suite 3207
Sacramento, CA 95814-5901**

Or fax completed order form to: **916-323-0823**

Note: Mail orders must be accompanied by a check, a purchase order, or a VISA or MasterCard credit card number, including expiration date and your signature. Purchase orders without checks are accepted from educational institutions, businesses, and governmental agencies. Purchase orders and credit card orders may be placed by FAX (916) 323-0823. Telephone orders will be accepted toll-free (1-800-995-4099) for credit card purchases. Please do not send cash. Stated prices are subject to change. Please order carefully; include correct item number and quantity for each publication ordered. All sales are final after 30 days.

R03-016 402-0215-656 10-04 5M

My Best Friend

Mary Ann Rodman

Illustrated by

E. B. Lewis

PUFFIN BOOKS

PUFFIN BOOKS
Published by the Penguin Group
Penguin Young Readers Group, 345 Hudson Street, New York, New York 10014, U.S.A.
Penguin Group (Canada), 90 Eglinton Avenue East, Suite 700, Toronto, Ontario, Canada M4P 2Y3
(a division of Pearson Penguin Canada Inc.)
Penguin Books Ltd, 80 Strand, London WC2R 0RL, England
Penguin Ireland, 25 St Stephen's Green, Dublin 2, Ireland
(a division of Penguin Books Ltd)
Penguin Group (Australia), 250 Camberwell Road, Camberwell, Victoria 3124, Australia
(a division of Pearson Australia Group Pty Ltd)
Penguin Books India Pvt Ltd, 11 Community Centre, Panchsheel Park, New Delhi - 110 017, India
Penguin Group (NZ), Cnr Airborne and Rosedale Roads, Albany, Auckland 1310, New Zealand
(a division of Pearson New Zealand Ltd)
Penguin Books (South Africa) (Pty) Ltd, 24 Sturdee Avenue, Rosebank, Johannesburg 2196, South Africa

Registered Offices: Penguin Books Ltd, 80 Strand, London WC2R 0RL, England

First published in the United States of America by Viking, a division of Penguin Young Readers Group, 2005
Published by Puffin Books, a division of Penguin Young Readers Group, 2007

3 5 7 9 10 8 6 4 2

THE LIBRARY OF CONGRESS HAS CATALOGED THE VIKING EDITION AS FOLLOWS:
Rodman, Mary Ann.
My best friend / Mary Ann Rodman ; illustrated by E. B. Lewis
p. cm.
Summary: Six-year-old Lily has a best friend for play group day all picked out,
but unfortunately the differences between first-graders and second-graders are sometimes very large.
ISBN: 0-670-05989-7 (hardcover)
[1. Best friends-Fiction. 2. Friendship-Fiction.] I. Lewis, Earl B., ill. II. Title.
PZ7.R6166My 2005
[E]-dc22 2004022778

Puffin Books ISBN 978-0-14-240806-3

Manufactured in China
Set in Coop light
Book design by Nancy Brennan

For Lily Nell Rodman Downing and David Eley
—M. A. R.

To the children of the Hammonton Swim Club
—E. B. L.

Today is Wednesday. It's playgroup day at
the neighborhood pool.
That's when I see my best friend, Tamika.
Tamika is bigger than me. She's seven.
She wears her hair in cornrows with beads.
She has a two-piece bathing suit with pink
butterflies and three rows of ruffles.

"Hi, Tamika," I say.

Tamika wrinkles her nose and sticks out her tongue. Then she jumps into the pool with Shanice.

Tamika is my best friend. She just doesn't know it yet.

"Tamika is ignoring me," I tell Mama.

"Tamika is seven and you are six, Lily," says Mama.

"I'll be seven pretty soon," I say.

"But when you are seven, Tamika will be eight," says Mama. "There are lots of other little girls here. Why don't you play with them?"

I don't want to play with other little girls. I want to play with Tamika!

I bet Tamika would like me if I had a two-piece bathing suit.

"Mama, can I have a new bathing suit?" I ask. "Only babies wear suits with a whale on the front."

"Not until you outgrow that one," says Mama. "Plenty of wear left in that suit."

Mama isn't looking too close.

The very next Wednesday, Shanice yells,
"Hey, Whale Girl."

"Who, me?" I ask.

"Yeah, you," says Shanice. "Your be-hind
is hanging out of your suit."

I run to the bathroom and check
in the mirror. Shanice is right.

Next playgroup, I have a new bathing suit. It is just like Tamika's—two-piece, with pink butterflies and three rows of ruffles.

"Hi, Tamika," I say. "See my new bathing suit?"

"That's a baby suit," says Tamika. "I used to have one just like it."

Tamika has a new suit, too. It is a sparkly pink one-piece with circles cut in the sides, like bites out of a cookie.

"I like your new suit," I say. Tamika doesn't hear me. She's pushing Shanice into the baby pool.

"I like your new suit, Lily," says Keesha. Keesha is six, like me. She's nice, but she's not Tamika.

"Thank you," I say. That Tamika! How can I make her be my friend?

I try sharing. I split my Popsicle with Tamika.

She shares her half with Shanice.

I let Tamika borrow my floating noodle. Tamika and Shanice float away, pretending they are mermaids.

That Tamika! If Shanice weren't there, we could be real good friends.

Then one Wednesday, Shanice isn't there.

"Do you want to play mermaids?" I ask Tamika.

"OK," says Tamika.

We have so much fun, Tamika and me. We play mermaids. We slide down the slide. At snack time we share. I give her half of my cherry Popsicle. She gives me half of her grape one.

I am so happy I think I will pop. Tamika is my best friend.

I can hardly wait for next Wednesday.

"Tamika, where are you?" I call when I
get to the pool.
There is Tamika. And Shanice.

"Is that baby still here?"
Shanice yells from across
the pool. "Isn't it time
for your bottle?"

I want to stick out my tongue
at Shanice. Tamika, too. They laugh
and laugh. They think it's funny.

I am not a baby! I am so mad, I jump
into the pool.

"You are a good diver," says
Keesha. Keesha is nice, but she's not
Tamika.

"Thank you," I say. That gives me an idea. Maybe Daddy could teach me how to really dive. Maybe Tamika would like me if I could dive.

Daddy and I work and work. He shows me how to stand, hands over head, feet in the right place.

At first I just fall in, belly first, the way I always do.

Then one day, I do it right! Daddy scoops me up and hugs me. We laugh and laugh. All the time I am thinking I can't wait to show Tamika.

The next Wednesday, I run ahead of Mama.
Tamika is in the big pool with Shanice. They
are standing on their heads underwater.
"Tamika, watch this," I shout.

I stand straight and tall, toes pointing down. I dive, sharp and clean. It is my best dive ever.

I float to the top and look for Tamika. She isn't there. Tamika and Shanice are climbing up the pool ladder.

Tamika didn't see my dive.

"That Tamika," says a voice behind me. "She wasn't even looking."

It is Keesha.

"That Tamika and Shanice," says Keesha. "They think they're so big 'cause they're going into second grade."

"Yeah," I say.

"What's so great about second grade?" Keesha bounces up and down, making little waves.

"Yeah, what's so great about second grade?"
I bounce up and down, too.

"Do you want to play mermaids?" asks Keesha. She smiles so the space in her teeth shows. I wish I had a space in my teeth. Keesha is nice. Who cares if she's not Tamika?

"Nope," I say. "Let's play sea monsters. You got a noodle?"

"Yeah," says Keesha. "A blue one."

Maybe someday, when Tamika is a hundred and I'm ninety-nine, we'll be friends. But until then, Keesha and I will have lots of fun.